HOW TO BUILD A TINY HOUSE ON WHEELS STEP BY STEP

TINY HOME CONSTRUCTION, BUILDING, PLANS, & DESIGN

JORDAN LIBERATA

JORDANLIBERATA.COM

CONTENTS

Just For You!

A Free Gift To My Readers

This quickstarter is a gift to readers to apply what they learn in this book. Within this quickstarter are a task checklist, a budgeter, a location tracker, and a list of things not to do. Get yours now and make your tiny house dream a reality!

jordanliberata.com

INTRODUCTION

Wow, it's almost midnight, I thought to myself, *this is the third night in a row.*

It was another night of watching youtube video after youtube video, reading blog after blog, and scratching my head. I wasn't getting anywhere. I felt utterly consumed by the massive amount of information out there and yet entirely unprepared to build a tiny house. Why was I so stuck?

If you're anything like me, you've spent a lot of time trying to figure out what it takes to build a tiny house. And despite the overwhelming amount of information, the lack of clarity and instruction, and the noise surrounding half-baked information, you can build a house. You can build a better life. And you can do it without having to stumble your way through it armed with nothing more than a couple of blogs and some one-off videos.

If you're here, you are probably more than just dipping your toes into the world of the tiny house on wheels. You probably already know a good deal about them, about the intricacies of the tiny house movement, about how people are tossing aside the traditional mortgage anchor for a more liberated and debt-free life. But getting that independent life can seem complicated. Sure, you can buy a tiny house, but that's not all that feasible for most. It also comes with a lot of restrictions and not a lot of customization. You could, of course, have one built for you, but again, that's a lot of money to dish out on a property that doesn't gain value over time. Plus, the point is ultimately to find freedom, financial or otherwise, not just to live in a new and smaller house.

The third and final option, and why you are most likely reading this book, is to build it yourself. Many say that the things you make yourself are the most cherished and that the journey itself is half the purpose of any sort of life transformation. This book is here to help you make that transformation on your own, but without being entirely in the dark or lost along the way.

What you will find ahead of you in this book is a step-by-step guide--60 steps precisely--that will outline exactly how to design and build your perfect tiny house on wheels.

With that said, no such thing as *the* perfect tiny house on wheels exists, but *your* perfect tiny house on wheels does! Your perfect tiny house on wheels is one that meets your specific needs and those of your partner or family. It is a house that represents the transformation into a freer and ultimately happier life. It is a house that better connects you to nature if that is what you want. Or a house that enables you to roam, if that is more your style. Or a house that reduces your impact on the environment. Ultimately, it is a house that achieves a purpose. The tiny house on wheels is not the goal. It is the tool that enables you to reach your goal: a better life.

Like any tool, your tiny house on wheels should be a tool that is not only fit to the purpose at hand--in this case, living your life fully--but is also durable, safe, and with all its parts functioning. In this case, that means avoiding the pitfalls of first-time house builders, taking the necessary steps, and having a full view of what it takes to build a house, and perhaps more importantly, why those steps need to be taken.

I am a simple person. I have a strong desire to help people find financial freedom and to help people enjoy a better life. I have spent time off the grid, live a minimalist lifestyle, and have always pursued a life of simplicity and purpose. I am a lover of nature and adventure, and have always been a believer in and practitioner of DIY. I believe that if you plan correctly and get the proper guidance, you can achieve anything that you want to achieve. I am deeply passionate about the tiny house movement and, in my pursuits, have identified a burning need for people to logically and directly get thorough guidance. There is a lot of content out there. Some of it is good, and some of it is not so good. Regardless of quality, the majority of tiny house content does not focus on the overall picture. Content is often laid out like pieces to an unmade jigsaw puzzle, where the aspiring tiny house dweller is left trying to piece together all of the different things that make up a tiny house. This book is here to put together the pieces of that jigsaw puzzle for you, so you not only have a clear template when building your house, but you also know you didn't leave out any critical pieces when you finally finish your tiny house on wheels.

Think of this book as your extended checklist, with explanations throughout explaining what we're doing and why. You'll find diagrams and straightforward language that tells you exactly what you need to do. You'll understand everything from choosing a trailer to putting the finishing touches on your finished interior and everything in between. You'll understand how to build walls, protect physical structures, and keep yourself warm when it's cold and cool when it's hot. You'll learn how to manage waste, how to install plumbing, and how to collect water. You'll learn how to manage electrical power from the sun and backup power from other sources. You'll understand the details of how to control temperature and moisture, and you'll understand how to make a simple staircase and loft. Ultimately, you will learn what it takes to build a tiny house on wheels.

Without a doubt, there is more than one right way to build a tiny house on wheels. In fact, there are countless right ways. Likewise, and perhaps more importantly, there are countless ways *not* to build a tiny house. This book will explain the breadth of options in approaching your specific build, while simultaneously walking you through one of the many right ways to build a tiny house step-by-step. In essence, it will give you a holistic view of building a tiny house on wheels, so you don't end up building it in one of those wrong ways.

Whether you are an experienced DIY builder or new to construction entirely, you will learn the build process in a way that not only steers you clear of pitfalls but also explains everything in layman's terms. This book is not for contractors or electricians or plumbers. Instead, this book is for people who want to find a better life but just need help getting there. This book is the catalyst for the transformation you want to make.

Now, let's pick up the tiny house jigsaw puzzle pieces and start putting them together, one at a time.

1

HOW TO PREPARE & DESIGN YOUR TINY HOUSE

Before you even start to build your tiny house on wheels, you need to first prepare for it. If you are reading this book, there is a good chance that you have already spent ample time preparing yourself for this endeavor. Nevertheless, some concepts bear repeating. In this chapter, we will briefly touch on some of the big questions that need to be answered before building the tiny house, the importance of a plan and a team, as well as a comprehensive list of tools and materials required or suggested throughout the entirety of the build. Let's get right to it.

STEP 1: ASK YOURSELF THE BIG QUESTIONS ABOUT TINY HOUSES

Embarking on the tiny house journey is no small task. That said, it can be one of the most rewarding and life-altering decisions a person can make. When it comes to any sort of task, planning and preparing is the key. This book is going to help significantly in the building process, but one of my other books, Live Tiny & Be Free: Everything You Need to Know About Tiny House Basics, Living, Ideas, and Design, covers the details of the tiny house life in general, where a lot of the big questions get answered, specifically around tiny house basics, the downsizing process logistics, financing and insurance, legalities, and designing the space and systems. Before you begin the process of building your tiny house on wheels, you need a vision for what you want, why you want it, and how you plan to get there.

If you are reading this book, you have probably already determined that the tiny house lifestyle fits your needs, whether those needs are financial freedom, minimalism, adventure, environmental consciousness, connection with nature, or something else entirely.

Aside from knowing what you want and why you want it, the transition to tiny house life first involves understanding your budget from both the perspective of time and money. Take the time to sort this out.

Likewise, building a tiny house on wheels is more than just about building the house. It is all about having a better future, or at least a place to which you can escape. This need means understanding the laws in your country or state, especially related to the tiny house on wheels, usually treated as an RV. In this book, we will assume the most common restrictions: 13'6 x 8'6 (4.11 meters x 2.59 meters) and no more than 40 feet (12.19 meters) long, though more than likely you will use a trailer more in the neighborhood of 24 feet (7.31 meters).

It is also essential for you to know the location of the tiny house on wheels. If you are taking this on the road indefinitely to explore, then understand what climates you will be taking it to and think through how you will use it as an RV (though we will cover that in this book). On the other hand, if you plan to keep your tiny house on wheels stationary, then know exactly where you are placing it because that will dictate how you build the house. In general, we are taking the approach of being diligent in our plan to make the build go smoothly.

STEP 2: MAKE A DESIGN PLAN FOR THE SPACE

This book will walk you through step-by-step what you need to do, but that doesn't mean that you should start building the house before finishing the book. Instead, it is recommended that you read or listen to this book in its entirety before your build, then reference it as you go through the build process. Likewise, this book isn't intended to show you how to build a specific plan, as there is no one best version of a tiny house on wheels. Instead, this is a guide, so make sure you have a plan in place for your design before you begin the build. The projects that fail are the ones that never have a real plan in place.

You have options for finding a design plan, ranging from finding free plans online to purchasing robust plans. A simple google search can get you quite far. If you opt for this route, you get the benefit of not learning how to use design software, but you'll still need to understand the plan itself. The downside is that you are boxed into the design that you acquire.

Another option is to own the design process yourself. While you certainly can opt for the old-school pen and paper method, it is recommended that you take the time to learn simple design software. There are many good options out there to consider, all of which have a free version:

- ***Floorplanner***: this is very basic design software for beginners that will have you rendering floor plans in no time through drag and drop functionality.
- ***Sweet Home 3D***: this intermediate software enables users to design with dimensions and then convert mockups to blueprints.
- ***SketchUp***: this is the preferred option among builders, as it is excellent for designing from scratch if you are willing to spend the time learning how to use it.
- ***Some others worth checking out***: HomeByMe, DreamPlan, and The Sims

Aside from the floor plan itself, you'll also need to think about your system designs, precisely that of plumbing, electrical, and temperature control. Don't worry, we will cover these topics in-depth, so you know what you need to do!

STEP 3: GET YOUR MATERIALS AND TOOLS

There is nothing more frustrating than going to Lowe's or Home Depot multiple times a day or starting a project only to figure out that you don't have the right tools. We will refer to the materials and tools needed or recommended for each part of the process, but as you start the build itself, make sure you have your personalized list on hand. You don't need to have every single item for the entire build, but you should preemptively compile your tools and materials for the task at hand, such as building the walls or installing the plumbing.

Further, when buying materials like screws, nails, tubes, and wood, always buy more than you need. This approach will save you trips to the store. You can always make returns.

Tools and materials can get expensive quickly, so consider different buying, renting, or borrowing options. It is amazing, if not inspiring, to experience how helpful your community can be when simply asking people to borrow their equipment. When you give yourself ample time, you can also get creative with material, using recycled lumber, windows, and equipment. Expenses and time tend to be inversely related.

Again, this book will arm you with this information as we walk through each component of the build, but as you think about the linear steps that need to be taken, tools and material will always come first.

You could argue that all you need is safety equipment, a hammer, a handsaw, a tape measure, and a speed square, but the reality is that you are going to want to invest a little bit of money for better tools so that you build the house properly and efficiently. Here is a comprehensive list of the tools you will need to rent or buy, both in general and for specific portions of the build. In this list and throughout the book, all measurements are written using the imperial system with the equivalent metric measurement in parentheses. While the list is quite exhaustive, understand that your particular build may require additional or different tools, as explained throughout the book.

Accessories:

- Safety goggles
- Ear protection
- Leather workman gloves
- Leather five-pocket work belt
- Extension cords
- Utility knife and extra blades
- Workbench
- Pencils
- Chalk

Basic Tools:

- Cordless drill (drill & impact driver is even better)
- Drill bit set
- 25-foot (1.5-meter) locking tape measure
- 7-inch (.15-meter) aluminum speed square

- Hammer
- Basic Phillips head screwdriver set
- Drip-free caulking gun
- Chop saw
- Circular saw
- 4-foot (1.2-meter) level
- C-clamps (at least 2)
- Bar clamps (at least 2)

Leveling the Trailer:

- Transit level
- Bottle jack
- Pier blocks
- Scrap wood

Subfloor, Wall, & Roof Frames:

- Sheet metal
- 2x4 (35mm x 90mm) lumber
- 2x6 (35mm x 140mm) lumber
- Plywood sheets: ½ inch thick (12.7mm)
- Foam tape/gasket
- Sill seal
- Carriage bolts
- Screws & Nails

Loft:

- Joist hangers
- 2x4 (35mm x 90 mm) lumber
- 2x6 (35mm x 140mm) lumber
- 1x6 (19mm x 140mm) tongue & groove flooring
- Screws & Nails

Exterior Finish, Windows, and Doors:

- Windows
- Doors/door jambs
- Shims -- leftover from frame construction
- Low-expansion spray foam
- Plywood sheathing
- Ice and water shield
- Roofing screws/nails
- Roofing material/metal
- Drip edges
- C-channels
- House wrap
- House wrap tape/sheathing tape
- Mastic tape
- The siding of your choice

Electricity:

- Wire strippers
- Lineman's pliers
- Screwdriver
- Outlets
- PVC outlet boxes
- Lights/fixtures
- Switches
- Subpanel
- Breakers
- Romex cables of varying gauges
- Auger bit/spade bit
- Wire nuts/push connectors
- Nail plates
- AFCI and GFCI circuit breakers
- Copper grounding rod
- Sledgehammer
- Grounding acorn clamp
- Grounding electrode conductor
- RV plug: 50 Amp, 240 Volt

Solar Power:

- Solar Panels
- 2x4s (35mm x 90 mm) / solar panels mounts
- Breaker box
- Charge controller

- Deep-cycle lead-acid batteries
- Inverter
- Solar cable
- Scrap lumber for solar cabinet

Backup Power:

- Transfer switch
- Portable generator
- Cinder blocks/equivalent for generator enclosure

Propane Appliances:

- Propane tank(s)
- Regulator
- Copper piping
- Copper pipe fittings
- Pipe flaring tool
- Teflon tape
- Soap & Water
- Spray foam

Plumbing:

- Composting toilet
- RV water inlet
- Valves

- Water tank
- Pump
- Filter
- Water heater
- PEX plumbing - blue
- PEX plumbing - red
- PEX fittings
- PEX crimp tool
- PEX clamp tool
- PEX pipe cutters
- PEX bend supports
- Shower
- Shower moisture barrier
- Steel mesh for shower
- Mortar for shower
- Sink(s)
- Sink clips
- Putty
- ABS or PVC piping
- P-traps or HepvO valves
- Air admittance valves

Rainwater Collection:

- Gutters
- Roof rails
- Gutter protector
- Water storage tank

- PVC pipe
- Mesh filter
- First flush diverter
- Pump

Air Control:

- Spray foam
- Insulation material(s)
- Wheel well boxes
- Vapor barrier
- Passive air vents
- Hole Saw
- Exhaust vents
- Heating & cooling systems
- Smoke detector
- Carbon monoxide detector
- Propane detector
- Radon detector

Interior Wall, Ceiling, Floor, Stairs, and Decoration:

- Tongue & Groove plywood panels
- Nails
- Paint/stain
- Polyurethane seal
- ½-inch (13mm) plywood with a smooth finish
- Wood glue

- Wood screws
- Handrail
- Appliances
- Cabinets
- Furniture
- Decor

STEP 4: ASSEMBLE YOUR TEAM AND MAKE A PLAN

Many hands make light work, so assembling a team is very important. There are stories of people building tiny houses entirely on their own, but this is not recommended, especially considering certain parts of the job are unsafe without two to three people.

As you gather your team, you also need to make a plan which includes a timeline and a budget. Do you want to finish this in a week? A month? A year? The timeline matters, as it is just as much a part of the plan as the design itself. Holding yourself accountable to a timeline makes it much less likely that you cut corners or give up entirely.

As far as the building goes, well, that's what this book is all about. So, now that we have our plan, tools, materials, and team, we can finally get our hands dirty!

2

HOW TO BUILD THE STRUCTURE: SUBFLOOR, WALLS, LOFT, & ROOF

At this point in the build, you have done your planning, assembled your team, and decided to take the plunge into building a house for yourself. Perhaps unsurprisingly, we will start the build at its base with the trailer itself and then work our way up through the floor, the walls, the roof, and ultimately the inside loft. Throughout this chapter, you will learn how to build a safe and stable structure. By the end of this chapter, you will have built a frame and will be well on your way to placing a roof over your head as your tiny life starts to unfold. This notion may seem daunting at first, but we are going to move through it step by step, and you are going to learn everything it takes to build a strong frame with a roof. So let's get right to it.

STEP 5: UNDERSTAND THE BASICS OF A TINY HOUSE STRUCTURE

This concept might seem somewhat silly to cover, but it is vital to address what a house does and why. You have probably lived in a normal-sized house at some point in your life but may not have thought about how the house truly works. At the most basic level, we know a house is designed to protect us from the elements, provide comfort, and give us a place to eat and go to the bathroom.

In the days of our ancestors, this "house" looked something like a cave with a wild boar roasting over a fire, maybe some furs for additional comfort and warmth, and a place to go to the bathroom outside of the cave. These basic needs haven't changed, but how we meet them has. We now have temperature control, power, cooking, appliances, decoration, and plumbing to satisfy these basic needs in a more advanced way. In doing so, we have more complex problems to deal with, but the core of what we are trying to achieve remains the same.

Namely, we have walls built of materials that are not rock. Rock is easy to deal with, but that is not realistic for most homes as a material, and especially is not in play when it comes to a tiny house on wheels where weight matters. While you could build a tiny house out of steel, it is easier and more common to make it out of wood, which we will explore in this book.

That means that we have to build the structure out of wood and protect that wood from damage, all while implementing systems for water, waste, power, and air control. At its core, that's all a house is. As we cover the intricacies of the subfloor, walls, and roof--both in this chapter and beyond--we will always think about the fundamental need to protect the structure itself from the elements.

STEP 6: ACQUIRE YOUR TRAILER

There are different options for the trailer that you can use, but generally speaking, we will look at a trailer in the range of 8.5 feet x 24 feet (2.6 meters x 7.3 meters). Some trailers are wider than 8.5 feet (2.6 meters), but it is strongly recommended that you avoid these unless your trailer is being delivered directly to the place where your tiny house on wheels will reside permanently. This is because the laws surrounding trailers wider than 8.5 feet (2.6 meters) make transportation impractically expensive. As far as length goes, stick to a trailer under 30 feet (9.1 meters) long. The longer the trailer, the heavier it is and the more challenging it is to tow. Plus, laws vary but generally prohibit the total length of the trailer and truck to exceed 53 feet (16 meters). Since trucks range from about 20-23 feet (6-7 meters), a 30-foot (9.1-meter) trailer is the maximum. Tiny house residents that are mobile opt for shorter trailers, while families and non-mobile residents tend to choose the longer ones.

Once you have figured out your desired length, you can figure out the type of trailer you need. There are a handful of options, the most common being the utility trailer, which has wheel wells above the deck floor and typically measures 8 feet (2.4 meters) wide. The most common lengths of utility trailers are 20 feet (6.1 meters), 24 feet (7.3 meters), and 30 feet (9.1 meters). The utility trailer is the most common choice due to its low deck height of only 18 inches (45 centimeters) above the ground. Tiny houses on wheels can only be 13.5 feet (4.1 meters) tall, so you want a trailer that doesn't sacrifice vertical space.

There are other options worth considering. The gooseneck trailer enables the house to be built over the truck bed but has a deck height of 32 inches (81 centimeters) above the ground. The deck over trailer option is 30 inches (76 centimeters) above the ground but lacks the bump over the truck bed. Its advantage is a simpler building process because there are no wheel wells. As we will explore, the wheel wells are much less painful than they might first appear.

The diagrams and descriptions in this book are based on the utility trailer, but you can apply the build concepts to whichever trailer you choose.

STEP 7: LEVEL THE TRAILER

Your trailer is your foundation, and thus, working with a level trailer is paramount throughout the entire build and must not be overlooked. First, you need to find level ground. Use the trailer's tongue jack (if one exists) to crank the trailer to level. The tongue jack is the first step in leveling, getting us to a decently level position. Next, we will dial in the precision for a perfectly level surface.

If you are building in a warehouse or other form of a concrete surface, you likely already have relatively even surfaces to build on. If you are building on grass or dirt, then dig down to bare earth. In either case, find four points around the trailer, two on each side about 25 percent of the way in from the end of the trailer. We will place support structures directly under the trailer frame at each of these four points, ensuring that the load is supported evenly. Do not jack up the trailer so that the wheels are off the ground because that is not how trailers are meant to support weight. This is a common mistake among builders and one you want to avoid.

Level each of your four points. Place conical pier blocks with 18-inch (46-centimeter) bases and 10-inch (25-centimeter) tops at the four support points. Again, check that this is level. Next, stack blocks of wood (4x10s work well) onto the pier blocks until there is no space left for another block of wood. At this point, you are ready to level the trailer with great accuracy.Unfortunately, a string level or regular level is not sufficient. Remember that if our foundation is not level, the whole build will be difficult and potentially unsafe. For this reason, rent or borrow a transit or laser level, and set it up pointing at the trailer. Now use the bottle jack to make the trailer precisely level. As with any equipment, keep safety in mind and follow proper use instructions when operating the bottle jack. Place custom cut blocks or shims between the blocks and the trailer, now that it is level. When you remove the bottle jack, your trailer will rest level on the pylons and blocks. Do not build on top of bottle jacks; this is dangerous and unreliable.

You will also need to level the trailer after the floor is built, before raising the walls.

STEP 8: BUILD AND ATTACH THE SUBFLOOR

Now that the trailer is level, we can begin building the subfloor on the trailer. This is relatively straightforward. First, prep the floor. You don't need all the deck boards, and since weight is very important in a tiny house on wheels, consider removing half of the boards. Next, attach sheet metal on top of the deck boards using lath screws. This sheet metal will protect your tiny house from the elements when on the road, as well as animals. Wherever there are seams between pieces of sheet metal, install a foam gasket to seal the seam.

Once the sheet metal is attached, the subfloor framing can begin. Assembly of the floor is relatively simple, but make sure you consider the wheel wells and the length of your trailer when designing the subfloor. As you will see with the remainder of our build, we will be using 2x4s for the vast majority of our structure to save weight. 2x4 framing is just as structurally sound as conventional 2x6 framing techniques. The frame will have the 2-inch edges of the 2x4s in contact with the sheet metal, with the 4-inch edges running vertically (see Diagram 1). Use 24" on center construction, meaning: each joist running horizontally across the trailer is spaced 24 inches (60 centimeters) apart at the center of the joist. Lastly, be sure to leave a half-inch (1.3

centimeters) between the trailer side and the frame exterior, as this will leave space for the wall sheathing later in the build.

Diagram 1

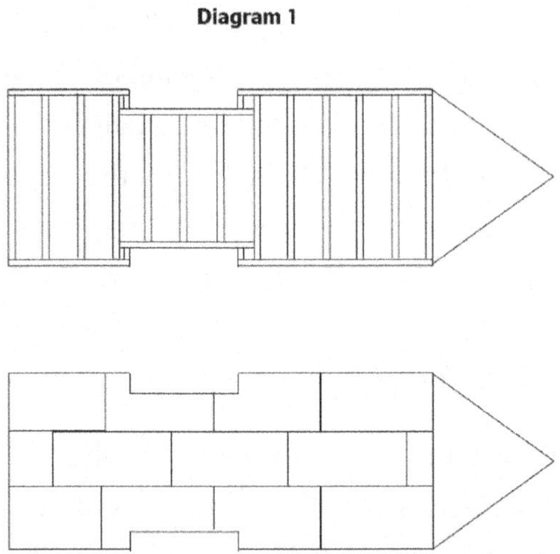

Assemble the subfloor on the ground. Consider building them in three separate parts to accommodate the wheel well and then screwing them together.

Next, mount and center the subfloor on the trailer. To attach it, countersink and drill a carriage bolt through the floor and sheet metal, then tighten the bolt on the underside of the trailer.

Once the subfloor is secured, cut installation to match the frame and install. Be mindful of any plans you have for drainage and plumbing that might be affected by the subfloor. While you can always pull up the floor later, it is best to avoid surprises by planning ahead.

Lastly, secure ¾-inch (2-centimeter) thick tongue and groove plywood panels to the subfloor using galvanized nails and subfloor adhesive. We will later stain these panels instead of adding additional flooring, as it will be lighter and just as comfortable. Since the subfloor will be exposed within the completed house, it is important to consider aesthetics by centering the panels.

Once again, level the structure using the previously explained method.

Your tiny house floor is now ready for walls and a roof!

STEP 9: FRAME THE WALLS

The walls will be different depending on your trailer dimensions and the type of roof that you are building. In this build, we explore the shed-style roof on a utility trailer, which is standard and uncomplicated. Given the laws in most places and the dimensions of a utility trailer, we must maximize our vertical and horizontal space. You will need to determine the type of roof you want and then design your walls to match that roof style. Step 13 will cover everything you need to know about roofs.

Diagram 2

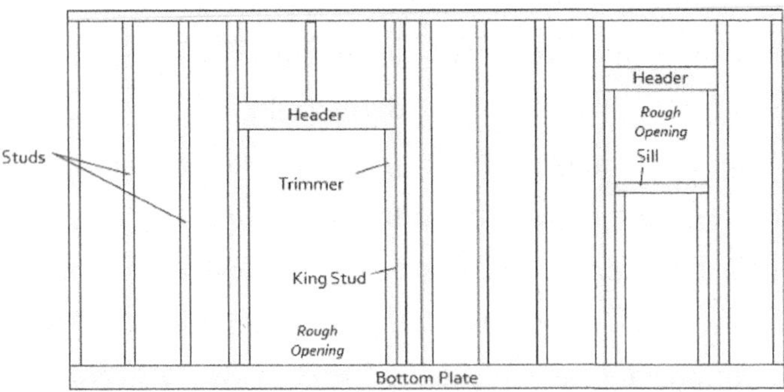

As far as the wall frames, use Diagram 2 as a reference for your build and sketch plan. In all cases, we will minimize weight by using 2x4s. Headers will be two 2x4s with a ½-inch (1.3-centimeter) piece of plywood sandwiched in the middle of them. It is also key that the studs above and below windows are flush. Be sure to account for the windows, doors, and wheel wells in your frames. Note that we will cover the insulation and covering of the wheel wells from the inside in a later chapter. We will address windows and doors shortly, but understand that certain sizes are standard, and custom windows and doors can get expensive, so be sure to plan accordingly when framing the house. Additionally, understand the difference between the door or window size and the rough opening of the door or window. The rough opening is the space created by the frame, into which you will place your window or door. For windows, the rough opening should be about ½-¾ of an inch (1.3-1.9 centimeters) wider and taller than the window. For doors, the rough opening should be about 2-2.75 inches (5-7 centimeters) taller than the door and 2 inches (5 centimeters) wider, but follow the manufacturer's instructions. Aside from the size and utility of the windows and doors, think about safety. It is strongly recommended that you build an egress window from the loft so that you can escape in the event of a fire or other emergency. Some tiny house builders also choose to have two doors, both for safety and a better flow of people.

Frame your studs 24 inches (60 centimeters) on-center rather than the conventional 16 inches (40 centimeters) on-center. This method is called advanced framing and is a perfectly reliable way to build a tiny house. This method of building is prevalent because it significantly reduces the weight, simplifies the build, reduces the environmental impact and waste, and improves insulation and associated energy costs.

Now that you have a sketch for the four walls, make a cut list. Making a cut list means simply compiling all the cuts you need before going shopping for your lumber. Don't just bring your sketches to the store. Make a plan, and you will save yourself much more time in the long run. Buy or acquire your wood and get some extra while you're there! Be sure to include the plywood panels that will cover your frame as well.

It is now time to start building the frames themselves, which should be done on the ground, as creating the frames directly on the trailer is more complicated and less reliable. Assemble by screwing the boards together first, which provides pull strength, followed by nailing the boards, which offers sheer strength.

A final key consideration is squaring the frame, as this will result in a solid and safe structure. Squaring is accomplished by measuring the diagonals from corner to corner. If the two diagonals don't match, go to the longer diagonal and push its corners together until they do match.

The last step is to mount the bottom row of plywood panels onto the frames of the two side walls, which are the longer walls. While this is certainly not necessary, it helps maintain the squared frame's shape while also making the attachment of panels easier. In addition, the bottom row of plywood should extend below the wall frame so that it can later be attached to the subfloor (see Diagram 3).

Diagram 3

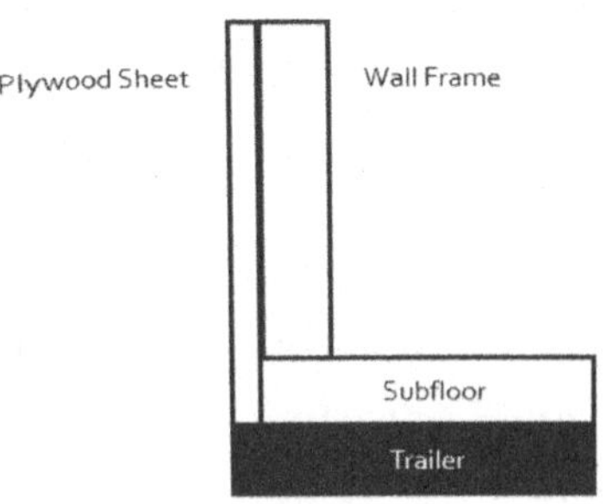

STEP 10: ERECT THE WALLS

Erecting the walls is a two or three-person job and should be done with caution considering the risk of a frame falling and being damaged or injuring someone. First and foremost, level the trailer again. Leveling should occur during all major parts of the build. To properly erect the wall, you will first need to staple a foam gasket called sill seal to the edges of the floor, which ensures a tight fit between the subfloor and the walls. Next, make a chalk line that identifies exactly where the inside of each wall frame will sit on the subfloor. Mount the longer and taller wall vertically and make sure that it is appropriately positioned on the chalk line. Also, make sure that it is relatively plumb, which essentially means that it makes a ninety degree angle with the subfloor and the earth. Once in place, brace the frame by nailing a 2x4 to the frame and securing it at an angle (See Diagram 4). Bracing is done for accuracy and safety reasons, so use common sense when determining how many braces you need. Finally, nail the bottom row of already attached plywood to the subfloor.

Once the longer and taller wall is upright and secured, it is time to move onto the longer and shorter wall. Repeat the same process as before, then continue to erect the end walls.

Diagram 4

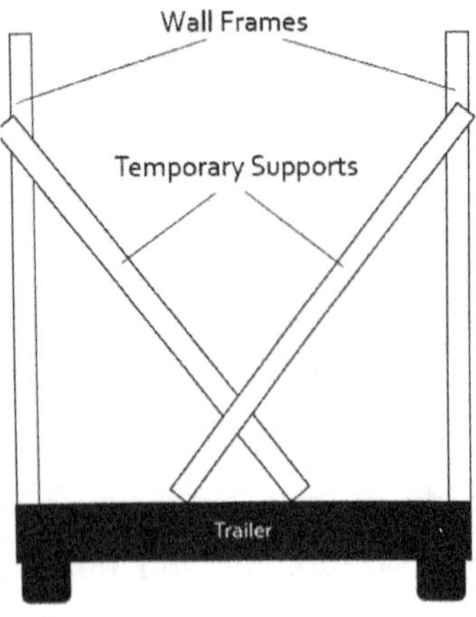

Now that all four walls are up, it is time to add the top plates, which are the wood boards that frame, connect, and plumb the tops of the walls. The top plates are 2x4s as well, and they are attached such that they stagger the seams, meaning that the seams of the connections between the sidewalls and end walls are covered (see Diagram 5).

Once the top plates are secured, remove the braces.

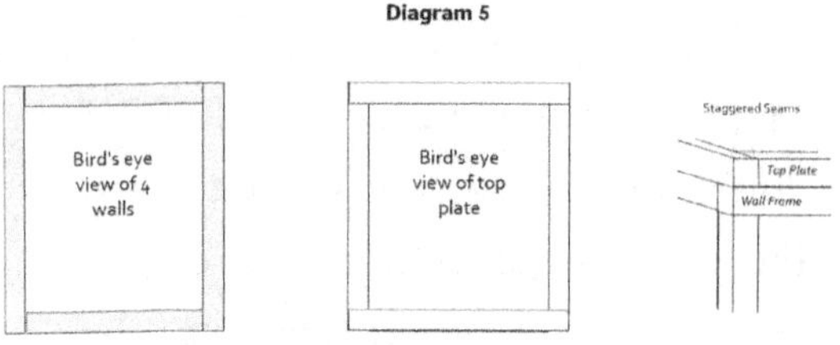

STEP 11: SHEATH THE WALLS

Finally, it is time to add the remainder of the plywood, which is known as sheathing. The plywood on the end walls should cover the frames of the sidewalls, meaning that the end of the plywood panel is flush with the sidewall panel.

Attach the panels from bottom to top using nails, and be sure to stagger them so that the vertical seams of the adjacent rows are not aligned with each other.

An easy way to deal with windows and doors while sheathing is to cover them entirely, then expose the rough openings. This is achieved by drilling holes in the corners of the windows and doors, then chalking lines connecting the holes on the outside and cutting out the plywood.

STEP 12: INSTALL THE HALF-LOFT AND INTERIOR WALL FRAMES

Upon completing the exterior, it is time to install the half-loft, more commonly called the loft. While many use the loft for sleeping, you do not have to. Many within the tiny house community complain about sleeping in their tiny house loft because they need to go up and down stairs--or worse, a ladder (which we will avoid)--to go to the bathroom.

You might wonder: if I'm not sleeping in my loft, where would I sleep? Some different options include bed-couch combination furniture, a retracted bed or Murphy bed, a roll-out bed that sits under an elevated kitchen, and even an elevator bed that can ascend and descend using pulleys. A quick google search will get the creative juices flowing if you're still unsure.

In either case, a loft offers a lot of utility by effectively expanding your floor space by about 40%. Of course, your loft's size will depend on the use of the loft, but a typical length is in the 8-11 foot (2.5-3.4 meter) range.

As far as the height of the loft goes, you should start by thinking about the headspace you want at the top of the loft. Typically, tiny house owners choose 3-4 feet (.9-1.2 meters) of headspace, but that can change depending on the utility of the loft itself. Given the interior dimensions of a tiny house on a utility trailer, the loft floor should be about 80-84 inches (2.03-2.13 meters) above the main floor, while the loft joists should rest about 76-80 inches (1.93-2.03 meters) above the main floor.

Now that you have designed your loft, the first step in the loft assembly is installing a horizontal 2x6 beam across the sidewalls. Make sure that the beam is level. Next, mount 2x4 galvanized joist hangers to the beam, 16 inches (40 centimeters) on-center, then mount the 2x4 joists in the hangers (see Diagram 6). Lastly, screw lightweight 1x6 tongue and groove flooring into the joists to complete the loft.

Now is also an excellent time to install any interior wall frames you may have planned for your bathroom, storage, or otherwise.

Diagram 6

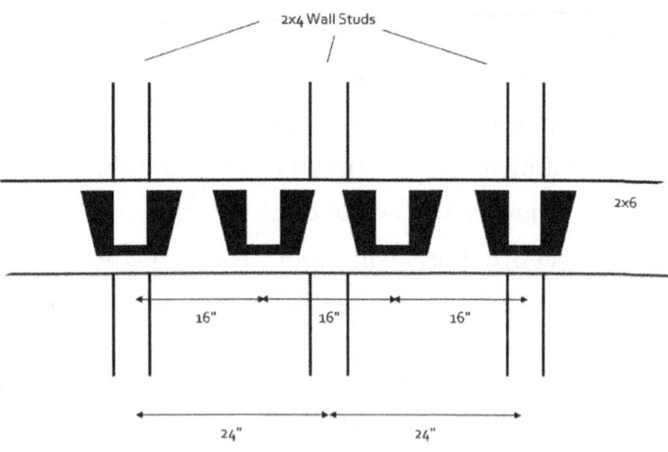

STEP 13: BUILD THE ROOF

There are many different options for the roof and various reasons to choose each. The most common are the gable and shed roofs, as they each have a different balance between ease of the build and maximizing vertical space.

Shed roofs can be built such that one side is higher than the other, or such that the front is higher or lower than the back. Many choose the front to back option because it maximizes loft space. Others prefer the side-to-side option because it enables one large wall that can provide ample sunlight. Shed roofs can have some difficulties handling snow removal, but are generally the simplest to build.

The gable roof is also quite common with tiny houses, as it is relatively simple to build while also providing headroom. It is the roof that has a centered ridge with two symmetrical sides sloping downward. A few downsides to it is that both walls are low and snowy climates may require more reinforcement. A saltbox roof is another viable option. It is somewhere in-between the shed and gable, having an off-center ridge and asymmetrical sides.

Diagram 7

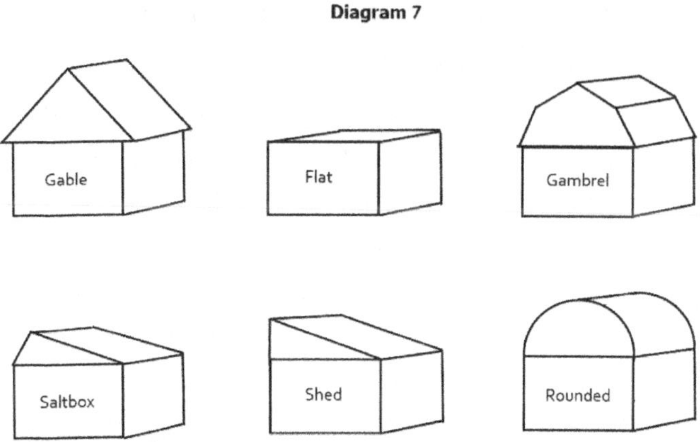

Some other options can be visualized in Diagram 7, but they are not recommended for a tiny house on wheels given their complexity and weight (in the case of the rounded and barn roofs) or their lack of durability to the elements (in the case of the flat roof).

In this specific build, we will keep it simple with the shed-style roof. If you are building a gable or saltbox roof, you will first need to build and install your ridgepole, which is the apex of the roof on which the rafters will sit. One of the benefits of the shed-style roof is that the taller wall--which is already built--acts as the ridgepole, making the build much more straightforward.

Cut the rafters to length using 2x6s. Rafters should overhang the edges of the walls about 2-6 inches (5-15 centimeters). While more length protects the structure better, it also adds weight and horizontal width on the road, so find a balance that works for you.

Diagram 8

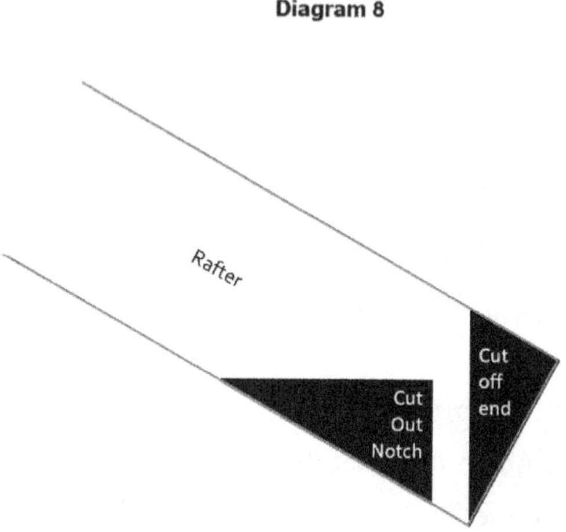

Rafters will be placed at 24 inches (60 centimeters) on-center, just like the wall frames. You will need to cut the ends of the rafters so that they will be perpendicular to the ground. You will also need to cut angled notches in the rafters such that they rest snuggly on top of the top plate of the walls, as shown in Diagram 8.

Next, add plywood sheathing to the roof with ½-inch (1.3-centimeter) plywood. Add from top to bottom and stagger, so the vertical seams do not line up on each row. Once the plywood sheathing is complete, install a metal drip edge on the roof's lower edge, as this will protect the structure and help water flow properly.

It is now time to protect the roof from the elements. To do this, we use ice and water shield, which keeps water out of the structure. In all aspects of your build, protecting the structure from the elements is paramount. Follow the manufacturer's instructions for applying the ice and water shield, but be sure to install from bottom to top with overlap so that water cannot penetrate the seams. Once this membrane is installed, you need to install a metal drip edge on the higher edge of the roof. We install the lower drip edge, then the ice and water shield, and then the upper drip edge because water flows downhill. This way, the upstream layer is always on top of the downstream layer.

Finally, it is time for the roofing itself. Don't even bother with shingles or anything fancy. Your tiny house on wheels needs to be lightweight and functional, which is why we will use metal roofing. There are a few different options for the type of metal roofing, though for most builders, steel is the best option:

- ***Steel-standing seam*:** This option has many color choices and reflective options, has a high life expectancy, and is suitable for collecting drinkable water, but it can appear industrial and may be challenging to acquire.
- ***Steel through-fastened panels*:** This option is inexpensive, has color options and wind resistance, is easy to install, and is suitable for collecting drinkable water, but it can have a short life expectancy, lacks expansion and contraction, may need sealant, and isn't suggested for roof pitches under 3:12. The roof pitch of 3:12 means that for every 12 inches of horizontal distance, the roof rises 3 inches.
- ***Steel shingles*:** These are easy to install and energy-efficient, are suitable for collecting drinkable water, have reflective pigments, a long life expectancy, and can look good to the eye, but you will likely pay extra for these benefits. These aren't suggested for roof pitches under 3:12.
- ***Aluminum options*:** There are different

aluminum options out there. Generally, these are good for salty and damp climates and last a long time, but they are more costly.

- ***Copper and Zinc options***: These options are weighted decently, wind-resistant, and quite attractive, but they aren't suitable for rainwater catchment, require professional installation, and are costly.

Install the metal roofing with a 1 inch reveal past the bottom drip edge, which means that the roofing hangs over the bottom edge slightly. As with all steps in your construction, make sure this is square. Unless noted otherwise by the manufacturer, use roofing screws to install the roofing because they will seal the hole that is drilled into the metal quite well. At this point, we are ready to move on to finishing the walls. Note that we will cover gutters and rain catchment for sourcing drinking water later in the book.

At this point, you will have achieved an incredible feat: building the structure of a house. When it's all said and done, it isn't particularly difficult. Like most big tasks, it is just a matter of putting the pieces together and taking it a step at a time, all while remembering the fundamentals. In this case, that means remembering the importance of a level structure, the importance of your frames being square, and building a house that suits you best. Now that the most labor-intensive work is done, it is time to protect your beautiful structure from the elements.

3

HOW TO FINISH WALLS AND EXTERIOR: WRAPPING, WINDOWS, DOORS, & SIDING

In this chapter, you will get the guidance needed to protect the structure that you just built in chapter two. It is always important to remember that the idea behind a house is as much about protecting the inhabitants as it is about protecting the structure itself. If the frame were made of rocks, it would be very straightforward, but it is not! We have a lightweight frame built of wood, which means we need to protect that wood from the elements. That means anything and everything from water and air, to dust and dirt, to snow and wind. By the end of this chapter, you are going to have a bulletproof structure that is safe, durable, and comfortable. Let's get to it!

STEP 14: WRAP THE HOUSE

House wrap--also known as a water barrier or weather barrier--is a critical component of a tiny house. If you are new to construction, you still have probably seen house wrap, or its well-known brand, Tyvek, whenever you see active construction projects in your area. The whole purpose of house wrap is to prevent moisture from becoming trapped in the walls. Water can damage the lumber of your frames, which reduces structural integrity. It can also lead to mold, which can be toxic and dangerous to your health.

House wrap functions in two distinct ways. First and foremost, it keeps water from the elements out of the structure of the house, which is why we put house wrap on the outside of the wood frames we just erected. Secondly, house wrap is semi-permeable, which means that water vapor from inside the house can escape.

When considering which house wrap to buy, it is recommended you go with the more reliable yet more expensive Tyvek, as it is the industry standard. However, if you opt for something cheaper, then make sure you research how durable it is, how water and air resistant it is, its permeability, and its drainage.

To wrap the house, start in one of the bottom corners. Make sure that it is square when wrapping, and attach it with staples. Cover all of the rough openings of your doors and windows. If you have any nooks and crannies in your build, such as gables or sidewalls, make sure those are wrapped as well. We cover everything first because it takes less material in the long run and makes wrapping much more manageable.

After wrapping, you are ready to prep the windows. First, make a slit with your utility knife along the top edge of the opening of your window. Next, make 2-3 inch (5-7 centimeter) slits at about a 45-degree angle from the top right and left corners of your window. Then, from the center of the top horizontal slit, make a vertical slit toward the bottom of the rough opening, stopping about 5 inches (12 centimeters) above the bottom edge. Now, make slits *inward* from the bottom right and left corners of the window at about 45-degree angles. Finally, connect the ends of the bottom corner slits with a horizontal slit, meeting with the vertical slit (see Diagram 9). The top and bottom flaps are different because of the way that water flows down the side of a building. The top flap will be exterior to the window, while the other flaps are interior to it. This way, water does not get into the window opening.

Diagram 9

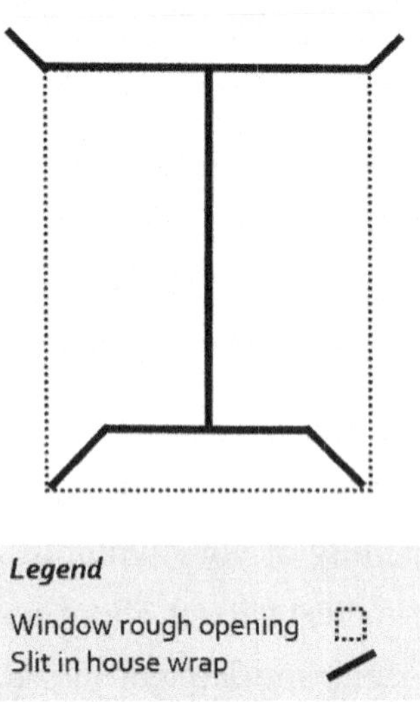

You now have two nearly identical side flaps, one bottom flap, and one top flap of house wrap. Tuck in and staple the two side flaps and bottom flap to the interior of the walls so that they are snug with the opening. At this point, your windows are prepped.

Now it is time to prep the house wrap on the doors. There are different styles and approaches here, but the goal is always to prevent water from getting behind the doors. To go through a preferred method, cut an opening of approximately 2 inches around the right, left, and top edges of your doors. Then, make slits of about 2 inches extending upward at 45 degrees from the top corners of the newly formed house wrap seam (see Diagram 10).

Diagram 10

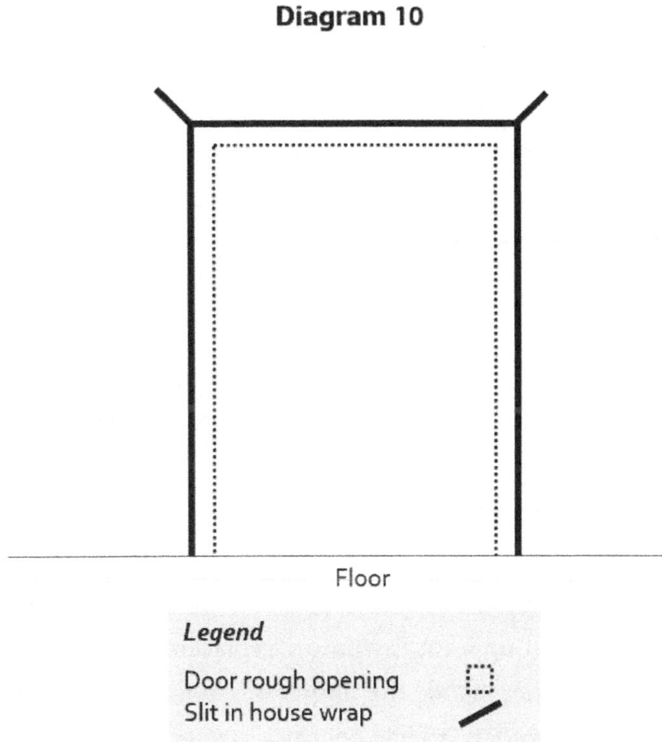

If you have any other openings that are already in place, apply the same methodology as the windows and doors, thinking logically about how the house wrap acts as a water barrier. If you only have windows and doors in place, that is completely fine, as we will cover all of the other wall openings later, such as plumbing and ventilation.

Lastly, tape the seams of all the house wrap using house wrap tape. You now have a structure with a proper weather barrier in place!

STEP 15: CHOOSE YOUR WINDOWS

With the rough openings of your windows completed and wrapped, you can go ahead and install your windows, but before installing them, you need to figure out what kind of windows are right for you. Windows can easily be one of the most expensive components of a tiny house on wheels, maybe except the trailer itself. If you are looking for ways to reduce your expenditures drastically, give yourself time to find repurposed windows. You can go to nearby construction sites to ask for scraps, find old windows at antique shops or places like Habitat for Humanity, or even call up a local window replacement company. On the other hand, the ability for your windows to properly insulate affects energy usage greatly, so more expensive windows may pay for themselves over time. Be sure to consider this when weighing your window options.

While windows have obvious aesthetic importance to your house, they also have different functions you need to consider. First, of course, you must consider if you want the window to open, and if so, how. Make sure at least two of your windows can open to help with air flow.

As far as the exact considerations of the window selection, you must first determine the type of window you need. This is because the type of window will change how air flows into the house. Awning windows, for example, hinge at the top of the frame and open outward, making them very good for rainy weather. Here is an overview of some of the most popular types of windows:

- ***Picture/fixed window***: These windows do not open at all. The benefits to these windows are affordability and lack of air leakage since these windows lack seals. The major downside is that they provide no ventilation. Even though we are going to cover how to install passive ventilation and exhaust ventilation, most people like the extra control and comfort an open window can provide.
- ***Awning window:*** This window hinges at the top of the frame and is pushed outward to a cracked position. They are affordable, operate well in the rain, and let light in well. However, they are poor ventilators, and they don't open fully, which may feel confining to some people.
- ***Double-hung window:*** This is the kind of

window that has a top and bottom section, both of which can slide up or down. These windows are very good ventilators, especially when the top section can slide down. The downside is usually the price.

- ***Common casement window:*** The common casement window has a right and left section or sash, one of which can open from the outside hinge. These windows can create nice airflow if the wind is blowing from the right direction, and they won't break the bank. The cons here are that they shouldn't be left open in the rain and that they may require an additional safety catch to secure the seal when shut.
- ***Double casement window:*** The double casement window is just like the common casement window, except it opens on both sides. These windows have similar pros and cons, though they are generally one of the more expensive types of windows.
- ***Center pivot window:*** The center pivot opens such that the window pane sits near the center of the frame when open. This design makes these windows fantastic for airflow regardless of the direction the wind is blowing. That said, they don't do well in the rain when open.
- ***Slider window:*** The slider window is similar to

the double-hung window, except it operates horizontally, and one of the sections is fixed. These are a favorite among those who don't want to install an exhaust fan in the bathroom because they can be made very small. The main downside is that they can get dirty pretty easily and are difficult to clean.

- ***Louvre window*:** This style of window consists of several horizontal panes each on its axle, which forms slits when open. They are good for airflow in both directions, and suitable for long and narrow spaces. However, they are not good for light or a view and protrude into the room, which can impede your space. They also can be a maintenance challenge.

Second, consider the ability of the window to resist moisture. This consideration mostly comes down to the window frame itself. Here are your different options:

- ***Vinyl window frames*:** This option is a favorite among many tiny house builders, as it provides solid value. Vinyl window frames are moisture-resistant and affordable, not to mention vibration-resistant. The two downsides are that vinyl windows easily scratch and are not particularly UV-resistant, which means they can break down in climates with lots of direct sunlight.

- ***Aluminum window frames***: This option is inexpensive, lightweight, and slim-line, meaning the frame itself is small in comparison to the windowpane, allowing for more light in a smaller rough opening. Unfortunately, aluminum window frames easily form condensation, easily scratch, reduce insulation effectiveness, and can be challenging to install. They also aren't environmentally friendly to manufacture.
- ***Wooden window frames***: The wood option is suitable for those looking for a more natural feel and something that can be repaired. They are not great for seasonal climates because wood expands and contracts a lot, and they also may require a bit of maintenance. If you choose to go with wood, make sure you pick lightweight wood.
- ***Fiberglass window frames***: This option is generally high-performing and the most moisture-resistant. That said, they are quite expensive.

Third, consider the insulation value and the windowpane itself. Unless you are in a hot climate, do not use single-pane windows as they are poor insulators. As far as the windowpane, be sure to go with tempered glass or laminated glass if your tiny house on wheels is going on the road with you. These two types of glass will help resist shattering or at least make shattering less dangerous. As previously mentioned, don't skimp on insulation for the sake of saving a buck, as this will likely cost you later.

Fourth, consider the size and weight of the window. Like everything in the tiny house on wheels, weight matters. As far as the size goes, think about the effect and placement of your window when it comes to passive solar heat. Since the tiny house is a small space, the sun can heat it pretty quickly. For example, if you lived in a cold climate and built a shed-style tiny house, you could make the taller and longer side of the tiny house have many windows and place it facing north. This would create a greenhouse effect that would make heating your house much easier in the winter.

Finally, consider the altitude rating of the windows. If you will be traveling, use high-altitude windows. Suppose you were to travel to a high altitude without the properly rated windows. In that case, the windows' seals might break, causing moisture to collect within the panes, ultimately leading to replacement. If you will be keeping your tiny house in one location, make sure you find properly rated windows for your given altitude.

When it's all said and done, your windows should suit your needs for their different purposes, and they should also match your style. Give yourself the time to find the right windows and make sure you plan your rough openings accordingly. The rough opening itself should leave a gap of about ¼-⅜ of an inch (½-1 centimeter) around all four edges of the window.

STEP 16: INSTALL THE WINDOWS

Now it's time to install.

Place the window in the rough opening. From the inside, use shims for plumbing and leveling the window to center it into the rough opening. You can cut scrap wood from your framing process to make shims the correct width (see Diagram 11).

Diagram 11

Once the window is in place, screw in the window from the outside. This is going to be temporary. Confirm that the window correctly opens, closes, locks, and unlocks. If it doesn't, make any needed adjustments. If it does, then use roofing nails or roofing screws to secure the window. The manufacturer may provide instruction here, but you likely won't have the instruction if you are using repurposed windows. Given the particular frame material (vinyl, wood, etc.), you will want to research the proper method to attach the window to the frame.

At this point, it is time to weatherize the window. The window is covering the house wrap on the left, right, and bottom edges of the opening, while the top edge is still exposed and the top flap of house wrap is still hanging loose.

You will need to use mastic tape that weatherizes the window. This waterproof membrane prevents water from penetrating the seams and rotting your plywood, in the event that water gets beneath the siding, which we have not yet put onto the tiny house. From the outside of the house, put a strip along the bottom edge of the window. We need to start at the bottom and work our way up so that water doesn't get into the seams of the tape. Apply the strip so that it covers the flange and is flush with the outer edge of the window frame at its base, where the flange and frame meet. Give yourself some extra tape on both sides of the window so that the tape extends about a foot beyond the imaginary line drawn by the left and right sides of the frame. Next, apply the mastic to the two sides so that the tape runs vertically and covers the extension of the bottom tape. It should also be butting up against the outer edge of the window frame. Finally, apply the top strip of mastic above the upper flange but below the top flap. Then, apply a second strip of mastic above the upper flange *and* the top flap of house wrap. A cross-section of the structure would show the following order from inside to outside: plywood sheath, window flange, first mastic strip, house wrap, second mastic strip. This ensures that water will be funneled away from the house rather than towards it, which is the name of the game in protecting the structure. Lastly, make sure any slits are covered with mastic as well. At this point, your structure is protected from exterior water at the windows.

Move inside of the tiny house on wheels, where we will finish the window with interior insulation. Your window is already level and the shims are in place, but it can't hurt to check again that it is level. At this point, you can take two approaches. One method is called chinking, where insulation is stuffed into the half-inch of space between the window and rough opening, which we will not cover here. A more reliable and preferred method is to use spray foam to fill the gap instead. It is cheap and not particularly difficult to work with, and it has both insulation value and air resistance. To insulate using the foam, first make sure that you are using the proper type of foam. You want to make sure you use a low-expansion spray foam that is made specifically for windows and doors, as this will not bend your window frame like the other high-expansion spray foams. Using the spray foam can and straw, fill the gap half full and allow it to cure for about half an hour. The reason we do this is that the outermost spray foam will need to be cut with a utility knife, but the exposed foam that we will be cutting off acts as an air barrier while the interior foam does not, similar to how a loaf of bread has an air-resistant crust but its interior does not. By filling the gap half full and allowing it to cure fully, we are enabling an air barrier to set inside of the foam, such that we will not cut it. After about half an hour, go back and do a second pass to fill up the rest of the gap. After it cures for a few minutes, cut any excess foam with your utility knife. Your windows are complete!

STEP 17: CHOOSE YOUR DOORS

Just like choosing the right windows, there are a handful of factors to consider when choosing the right door for your tiny house on wheels. You have many options, ranging from standard door installation to trimming and repurposing old doors to building your doors yourself. In all cases, your doors should take four things into account: weather, weight, security, and access.

From the standpoint of weather, a door needs to be insulated. Manufactured exterior doors already take this into account. However, interior doors are generally insufficient for handling the elements, even though their weight makes them a tempting option. If you choose to build your door yourself, make sure you use solid wood that is at least 1.75 inches (4.5 centimeters) thick, and make sure that any glass in the door is tempered and follows the guidance given regarding windows.

Weight is always important in your design. Your doors are no different.

As far as safety, make sure your door or doors are correctly placed, make sure that they have a deadbolt to prevent theft or burglary, and make sure that they are durable enough to travel on the road with you. Apply the same logic that was applied when selecting your windows.

Lastly, do not forget about access. An accessible door firstly means that your door fits your needs from a size and height perspective. It also means that you can get your interior belongings and furniture through the doorway when the time comes. Forgetting that you need to get things through the entrance is an easily overlooked obstacle but difficult to deal with when completing the interior. If your cabinets, furniture, or appliances can't fit through the door, you will likely need to disassemble them or buy new ones, which is a frustrating and costly problem that is easy to avoid.

STEP 18: INSTALL THE DOORS

Once you have purchased or finished building your doors, you are now ready to install them into the rough opening, for which we will apply a similar technique as we did with the windows.

Your house wrap on the doors is already prepared, as explained previously. There is a 2-inch (5 centimeter) gap between the edge of the wrap and the rough opening, as well as two 45-degree slits on the top corners. On the exposed plywood, apply a primer that will help the mastic stick better. Just like the windows, we will start from the bottom and work our way up. Create a pan on the bottom of the opening by laying mastic where the door jamb will go. Next, follow the same process that was used for weatherizing the windows by applying mastic to the sides, tops, and slits of the door, in that order. When weatherizing the top of the doorframe, remember to apply one strip below the house wrap flap and a second above the house wrap flap.

Check that the bottom and sides are level and plumb, respectively. If they are severely off, make sure that the trailer is level, then custom cut small shims to make them level. If the sides are slightly off, you will be able to use shims once the door is placed in the opening. Next, run a bead of silicone along the exterior wall edge of the rough opening. For preparing the bottom, apply a base of silicone that covers the mastic pan. Place the door jamb in the opening, and make sure it is secure. Also, make sure to remove any inserts that come with the door, as there may be extra pieces that are only there for securing the door in transit. Center the door within the rough opening, then use shims to level and plumb the door jamb. You want to have shims behind every hinge to give structure and strength to the door. To attach the jamb to the frame of the door, use 3-inch (7.5-centimeter) screws. Tuck them behind the weather stripping and screw them in so that they are hidden. Now close the door and make sure it closes properly. Check that the door is level and plumb. Also, make sure that the gap between the jamb and the frame is even all the way around. If it is not even, unscrew the door jamb and adjust accordingly. Finally, insulate using two rounds of low-expansion spray foam, just as you did on the window insulation. Complete the door insulation by following any manufacturer instructions for installing the doorknob and deadbolt.

STEP 19: INSTALL THE SIDING

The final piece to completing the exterior is installing the siding. The siding's purpose is to further shield the house from the elements, while also making your tiny house on wheels look good. There are many different options for siding, but we need to make sure that it is lightweight, durable, and safe. The ultimate choice you make will depend on your budget, your style, and your climate or climates.

Generally speaking, the top three materials are wood, vinyl, and steel. To determine what works best for you, consider the following factors:

- ***Curb appeal***: Your curb appeal isn't about resale value like it is in a modern house. Instead, it is more about making your house fit your style while also fitting the places it may go. If you are taking your tiny house off the grid, you probably don't have to worry about this too much, but if you are taking it on the road or parking it in a residential area, you need to consider how others perceive your house. If your house looks good, neighbors and, by extension, inspectors likely won't care that it is there, even though it might fall into a legal gray area. If your house looks out of place, it could cause the neighbors to make a phone call you don't want them to make.
- ***Towability and weight:*** The weight of your tiny house on wheels matters, even if you aren't going to tow it. Siding can add up to a half-ton of weight to your house, which means you will be sacrificing weight elsewhere. Likewise, your

siding needs to be able to handle the wear and tear of the road unless you are going to build it and keep it in one place. These factors are reason enough to avoid wood, brick, stucco, and shingles.

- ***Fire resistance:*** Tiny houses that catch fire can go up like a matchbox if they are not adequately fire-retardant. That means that fire can not only cause you to lose everything you built in a matter of minutes, but it can also put your life and the lives of others in danger. The siding is the first defense against fire and is especially important if you live in a dry or wooded area. If you choose to use wood, make sure it is chemically treated to protect against fire.
- ***Climate tolerance:*** The more frequent environmental events like snow, rain, hail, and drought, are also going to affect the siding choice. Think about how the material expands with temperature and how well it resists rot and moisture.

In choosing your material, you will find that most materials cost roughly the same amount, less than $10 per square foot. You can opt for wood options, like cedar, pine, and plywood; you can opt for metal options, like corrugated steel or aluminum; or you can opt for synthetic options like vinyl. Some builders mix and match siding to create a unique aesthetic. Despite the many different options, your safest bet is steel. It is the only material that does not have a clear downside in the build process. Its main deterrent is that its manufacturing process takes a toll on the environment. Otherwise, it is an excellent option because it is lightweight, affordable, handles weather and climates of all types, resists fire, requires very little maintenance, and is very malleable in its design. You can even purchase steel that looks like wood. Regardless, meeting all of the criteria above is unique to steel.

Once you have selected your siding, it is time to install it. The installation will certainly depend on the type of siding you choose but generally will follow the same principles we have followed all along in repelling the elements away from the structure. First, cut your siding to the sizes that you need. Then, cut and install the c-channels. This is a channel that goes up against doorways and corners of the house, such that the siding slides into the c-channel with its edge hidden from sight. Next, install drip edges on the tops of windows and doors. A drip edge is an angled piece of flashing that is easily installed on the top of the window frame. Its purpose is to direct the water outward as it flows down the siding. Now that the drip edges and c-channels are installed, go ahead and install the siding as instructed by the manufacturer. This process most likely means moving from bottom to top and drilling the siding into the exterior wall. In the event you have any sidewalls, make sure you install sidewall flashing to protect them as well. You have now finished the exterior wall!

Altogether, the steps covered in chapter three are an important part of the build. It is important to be deliberate and meticulous in these steps because these are the ones that will ultimately protect your house from long-term damage. From wrapping to siding, always consider the purpose of the build: to protect the frame from water and air. As long as you consider why you are taking these steps, follow the techniques provided, and have a plan, you will have built a fantastic house that can withstand the elements for years to come.

4

HOW TO GET ELECTRICITY & POWER

It is finally time for that which is feared: power. Electricity and power is a big subject and one that tiny house builders often find intimidating. The task itself is a challenge, no doubt, but we are going to break it down into bite-size pieces.

Despite this description, it can not be emphasized enough: safety must come first. Electricity is no joke, and when installed incorrectly, is extremely dangerous. Both in the build process and in your future life with self-installed electricity, you must never skimp on safety. After all, this house is a means to finding a stable and independent future. Don't put yourself at risk. This means, at the very least, hiring a licensed electrician to check your work. This could also mean simply hiring an electrician to do all of the work. For many builders, it is somewhere in the middle. Regardless of the ultimate decision you make, use this chapter to help you understand what steps must be taken and gauge whether or not you are comfortable and capable of taking them on your own.

Aside from the essential safety considerations, you should be happy to know that while the electrical is inherently dangerous, it doesn't have to be very intimidating. Electricity follows relatively simple principles that you will learn in this chapter and is much simpler than you might expect.

Through this chapter, you are going to learn how electricity works in general, how to design the flow of electricity through your home safely, how to install the wiring and the subpanel or breaker box safely, how to ground your house correctly, how to source electricity both on and off-grid, and how to use propane to backup and supplement your electrical power. By the end of this chapter, you are going to understand electricity and know exactly what you can do--and perhaps what you cannot do--to power your tiny house on wheels. Let's begin.

STEP 20: UNDERSTAND ELECTRICITY

Electricity is powerful but manageable. Many tools are helpful, but only three tools are essential when dealing with electricity: wire strippers, lineman's pliers, and a screwdriver. The components used inside your tiny house electrical system are not particularly complex either, as they mainly just include outlets and lights, switches, wires, and a subpanel/breaker box.

The difficulty in electricity comes more from the general nature of electricity. Specifically, electricity is unwavering; it flows when it can and only stops when it has nowhere else to flow. Electricity flows through conductors the way that water flows through a river. It will not magically stop flowing unless it has nowhere to go. This powerful nature of electricity makes it a safety hazard, and it is why each country has its own electrical codes that should be followed by anyone dealing with electricity. When you have your electrician check your work, they should check that you are up to code.

If all of this talk about the power of electricity has you considering hiring an electrician for the whole job, certainly explore that option. It is very common for tiny house owners to build their tiny house themselves but outsource all of the electrical work, which will usually amount to approximately $1000. Outsourcing to professionals will generally cost about $100 an hour, but this varies by location. Another common outsourcing option is the hybrid approach, where you rough in the electric, but the electrician wires the subpanel. This approach means that you do the basic work installing the wires and electrical boxes (which are where outlets are installed), but the electrician does the rest. This is a recommended approach for non-electricians, as it will significantly reduce the cost to a few hundred dollars but will also ensure safety. As far as sourcing the electricity itself, be it on-grid or off-grid, we will explore those options later in the chapter.

Regardless of the way you install your electricity--be it fully outsourced, partially outsourced, or not outsourced--you will need to achieve three key tasks:

A. Understand basic electrical concepts.
B. Determine the electrical demand of your tiny house.
C. Draw a circuit diagram and electrical map.

Task A is to understand basic electrical concepts, which is best achieved by simply understanding basic terminology. We will cover the most basic here, so you have a solid foundation. It is not comprehensive nor intended to make you an expert in electricity. If you want to get deep into the weeds of electromagnetics, consider doing some independent research. Until then, we will cover the basics and introduce more advanced concepts only as needed. Here are eleven basic terms and concepts to understand for complete beginners:

- ***Amps***: More formally known as Amperes, this is the measure of current through a conductor. In the analogy of a flowing river, the Amp measures the volume of water flowing down the river. The symbol for Amps is A.
- ***Volts***: This is the measure of electromotive force through a conductor, so it essentially measures how strong a current is. In the analogy of a flowing river, the Volt measures the steepness or pitch of the river. The symbol for Volts is V.
- ***Watts***: Wattage is the measurement of power. They are calculated by multiplying Volts by Amps. In the analogy of a flowing river, the Wattage is the rate or speed of the river. The symbol for Watts is W.
- ***Watt-hour:*** The measurement of work. This is the amount of electrical energy produced or used in one hour. The symbol for Watt-hours is Wh. It is often measured in kilowatt-hours, or KWh, which is the measurement of watts produced in one hour times 1000.
- ***Conductor:*** Something through which electricity can flow. The wires in your walls are the main conductors in your electrical system.
- ***Subpanel:*** Also known as a breaker box, the subpanel controls the inflow of electricity into

the tiny house and where electricity is distributed to various circuits.

- ***Circuit:*** The circuit is the flow of electricity. Practically speaking, the circuit is the set of wires and fixtures powered by the same flow of electricity. This flow is either allowed or denied by a breaker in the subpanel.
- ***Breaker:*** A breaker, or circuit breaker, is a switch that allows or denies the flow of electricity into a circuit.
- ***Switch*:** Something that connects, breaks, or changes the connection in a circuit. Your light switch is an example, as is the breaker in the subpanel.
- ***Direct Current (DC):*** DC power is one of the two main forms of electrical current. It only flows in one direction and delivers a consistent flow of voltage. It is the current that solar panels capture, that batteries store, and that many devices need. It doesn't travel over long distances well. We will cover DC more in this chapter as needed.
- ***Alternating Current (AC):*** AC power is the other main form of electrical current. It is current that alternates periodically over set intervals, enabling much more efficient travel over long distances. AC will be used when

electricity enters the tiny house on wheels. We will cover AC more in this chapter as needed.

STEP 21: DETERMINE YOUR ELECTRICAL DEMAND

Task B is to determine your electrical demand. This is first achieved by determining your needs. Will I have a washing machine? Where should I place my lights? Am I using electricity or propane for cooking? How many outlets should I have? How am I heating water? The best way to answer this question is to make a comprehensive list of everything you do that requires energy, regardless of what that energy will be. Think about your daily life, from how you cook to how you power your devices to how you stay warm or cool. Once you have this list, you will know what you need to research further, and you will be able to estimate your electricity needs with reasonable accuracy.

List in hand, it is time to consult some basic charts that will tell you the amount of electricity used to both start and run the appliance. These are often called surge watts and rated watts, respectively. A simple google search will reveal a litany of options for finding appliance power demand charts.

It is recommended that you make a table by hand or in a spreadsheet with the following columns:

- Column A: Appliance
- Column B: Running Watts (found by referencing an appliance chart)
- Column C: Additional Starting Watts (found by referencing an appliance chart)

Then, add the total running watts together for all appliances by finding the total of Column B. Now take that sum and add the highest value of the additional starting watts in Column C. Finally, multiply this number by 1.25 (or whatever your code determines is necessary) to give yourself some room for error in the load calculation. You have now identified the maximum load of your system and given yourself an extra cushion.

STEP 22: MAP YOUR CIRCUITS

Now that you know the maximum load of the entire tiny house on wheels, it is time to move to Task C, which is to draw your circuit map and electrical diagram. These will be dependent upon your specific needs. First, design the diagram of the switches, outlets, lights, and appliances in the house. You can draw your map with a pen and paper using the standard electrical symbols provided in Diagram 12.

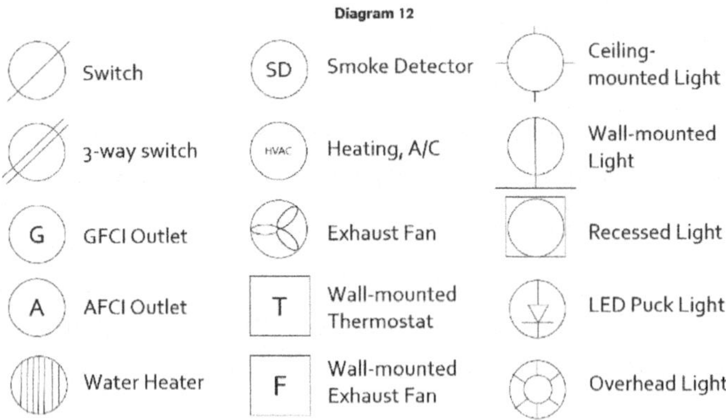

Next, you will plan the distribution of power by mapping your wiring. The concept is simple: power comes into the house in a single flow of electricity, hits the subpanel, and then flows through several circuits throughout the house. Each of those circuits is controlled by a breaker in the subpanel. You need to determine what those circuits will be, meaning you have to determine how to wire your house. A common tiny house on wheels is wired with the following seven circuits: kitchen, HVAC, loft, appliances, left-side main, right-side main, outside. While this is by no means the way you must wire your house, it should give you a sense of one way to wire it. The most important concept to remember in this circuit mapping exercise is that each circuit must tolerate its expected amperage, plus about 25%, depending on the electrical code that you fall under. Typically this means that your circuits will have a 20A circuit breaker, except for circuits with heavy draws, such as HVAC. It may be helpful to make a diagram or list where each circuit breaker is labeled, and underneath it is each electrical draw on that circuit. This will help ensure that you are correctly planning the demand of the circuit.

At this point in the process, you have successfully identified your electrical needs overall and by circuit. You have mapped where you want to install the electricity, and you have determined how electricity will flow once inside your tiny house.

It is now time to begin the installation process.

STEP 23: ROUGH-IN YOUR ELECTRIC

Roughing-in the electric, which is more or less equivalent to saying 'putting the wires in the walls,' is a piece that most amateurs can do or at least begin before outsourcing the rest. It consists of getting the proper wires, drilling holes in the frames, and installing the wires and electrical boxes.

The wiring is made up of cables. You likely hear the terms *cable* and *wire* used interchangeably, but technically, a wire is a single solid conductor while a cable is a bundle of wires. The standard type of cable used in tiny house design is Romex, also known as non-metallic sheathed wire. Romex comes in different forms, and those forms have different uses. The first number on the label is the gauge, and it dictates the size of the wire. The bigger the number, the smaller the wire. The second number on the label is the number of conductors, not including the ground. So, for a Romex labeled 12/3, its gauge is 12, and it has three conductors plus a ground wire. Typically, the following Romex can be used for different demands, but be sure the amperage is appropriately matched to the amperage that the circuit needs:

- Lighting Circuits: 14/2 Romex, 15 Amps
- Lighting and Outlet Circuits, & Refrigerators: 12/2 Romex, 20 Amps
- Electric Water Heater and Other Heaters: 10/2 Romex, 30 Amps
- Electric Clothes Dryer: 10/3 Romex, 30 Amps

When you strip your Romex, you will see the wires inside. For Romex cables with two conductors plus a ground, you will see a black wire for your hot lead, a white wire for your neutral lead, and a bare copper or green wire for your ground. For Romex cables with three conductors, you will see the same as the two-conductor cable, but with an additional red wire that is a second hot lead. Each wire plays a different role in the effectiveness and safety of wiring of the tiny house on wheels. We will explore these details further when wiring the subpanel.

Once you have your wires, it is time to rough them in. Take pictures and thoroughly map the wiring throughout this process so that you can later refer to the wires in the wall. We will be drilling through the walls later, so we need to know exactly where the wires are so we don't damage this work. Furthermore, a critical safety consideration and, in most places, code requirement, is to install electrical wiring above the plumbing. In the event of a leak, we do not want the safety hazard of water coming into contact with electricity.

The first step in the rough-in process is to install the PVC outlet boxes onto the sides of our wall studs, such that the box is flush with the wall. Use PVC outlets because they are much lighter, and they flex well with movement if the tiny house on wheels is mobile. Drill holes into the studs so the wiring can comfortably yet snuggly be pulled through. If the hole is too small, you risk damaging the cable; if it is too big, you unnecessarily risk damaging the structural integrity of the stud itself. Use an auger bit or a spade bit to drill through the studs. You may need a right-angle drill if you find yourself in a tight space as well. Mark the studs to indicate which circuit is being pulled through which hole.

Now that you have installed the boxes and holes, pull the cable through the holes and the electrical boxes, so that they stick out about 7 inches (18 centimeters) from the back of the box. Follow code here. Likewise, staple the wire according to code, which likely means stapling it every 4 feet (1.2 meters) and within 8 inches (20 centimeters) of the electrical boxes. Whenever you have more than two cables that need to be stapled, secure them using a stacker. It is important to be clean and organized with your cables to avoid future problems. If you need to connect two wires, use either a traditional wire nut or a push connector.

Lastly, install nail plates onto the stud in front of the hole. Nail plates protect the cables from nails and screws that get driven into the wall later.

Once you have pulled all the wires through, you have completed the rough-in. You are now ready to move on to the subpanel.

STEP 24: INSTALL YOUR SUBPANEL

Subpanel installation is not super simple nor super complex, but it is dangerous if done improperly, so consider outsourcing it. Regardless of whether you install it or a licensed electrician installs it, there are key steps to be taken and important considerations to be made.

As always, follow code throughout this process. First of all, the subpanel, which is also called your breaker box, is essentially the traffic control for the electricity coming into the tiny house. It is imperative that you only have 120 Volt loads in the subpanel and that you mount the subpanel in an accessible place. Use a breaker box with space for ten breakers.

Once mounted, remove the knockout slugs from the subpanel and bring in the wires. The neutral and ground will need to be bonded, so use a panel that has a bonding screw to make this bonding easy. The bonding screw is typically green in most subpanels. Next, route, cut, and strip the feeder wires and connect them to the terminals. These are the cables that are the source of your power. The subpanel should have two 120 Volt hot bus bars, which allows for 240 Volts to be delivered to the tiny house on wheels. The wire may vary in color, but hot wires are typically black, red, or white. Likewise, the subpanel has two bars for the ground and neutral (see Diagram 13).

Install breakers for each circuit. Tie the ground wires to the ground bar for each of the circuits. Sink in the bond screw, bonding the ground and neutral together. Next, tie in the neutral and hot wires into the breaker. The amperage of each breaker and its accompanying wires must match.

Diagram 13

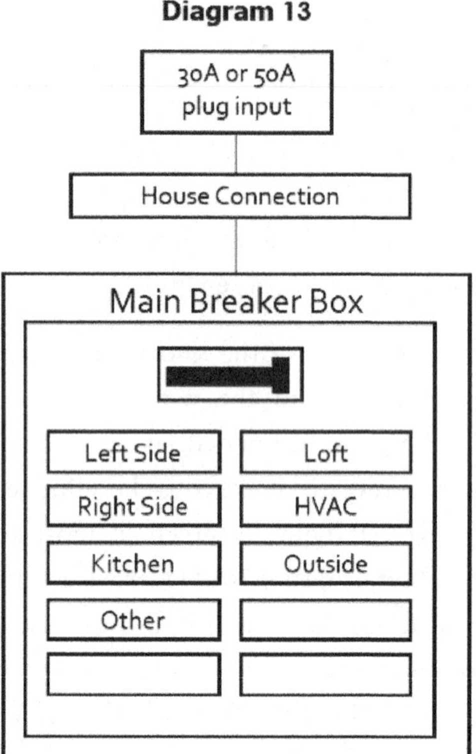

Furthermore, make sure you install AFCI circuit breakers and GFCI circuit breakers into your system. These breakers act as a line of defense in the event of an energy surge so that the circuits shut down when overloaded with electricity, thus preventing a safety hazard.

If you choose to wire the subpanel yourself, do your due diligence and take your time. It is simple but there is no room for error.

STEP 25: GROUND THE TINY HOUSE ON WHEELS

Once the rough-in and subpanel are complete, the tiny house needs to be grounded. Grounding is your last line of defense in case the electricity malfunctions. In essence, it allows excess electricity to escape safely into the earth. It is usually needed when there is a fault in the system's wiring. Still, it is an important security measure to take so that the ground absorbs excess energy, instead of the tiny house or the people in it. Follow code when completing your grounding.

For those keeping their tiny house in one location, grounding is achieved by providing a pathway into a copper rod driven into the ground. When electricity flows through this pathway, the rod carries the charge and disperses the electricity safely underground. Code will dictate if you need one or two grounding rods and the distance that they must be from the house.

First, put the grounding acorn clamp onto the first grounding rod. Use a sledgehammer to drive the first 8-foot-long (2.4-meter) copper grounding rod into the earth, at least 2 feet (.6 meters) from the building, or whatever code dictates. Install the second rod at least 6 feet (1.8 meters) away from the first, or whatever code dictates. Make sure you are not installing the rod where utility lines may run. Most countries have a hotline that you can call to have a locator check for lines. Connect a 6-inch-deep (15-centimeter) copper wire between the two copper rods, then tighten using acorn clamps.

Connect the grounding electrode conductor, which is the wire connecting the electrical system to the rod. Make sure there is a bit of slack, and the last half-inch (1 centimeter) or so is exposed wire. Backfill the trench to cover the copper wire.

If your tiny house on wheels is mobile, you will not be able to install grounding rods. Your main concern will be when plugged into the grid. The typical RV plug has a grounding pin in it, which means all you must do is test that the plug itself is operating correctly. While you certainly don't need to concern yourself with this at this point in the build, it is worth noting that there are methods for properly testing your electricity source, and you should do your due diligence once living on the road or connected to the grid. Rest assured, you will have options. One simple and affordable way to confirm that the RV plug is adequately wired is to use a multimeter, which is cheap and straightforward to use. If the source is not wired properly, find a new source of electricity so that you are properly grounded.

Finally, whether you are on-grid, off-grid, or both, you are now ready to connect the cables that feed the subpanel to the spot of the plug. It is recommended that you use a 50 Amp, 240 Volt, RV plug. You will need to install this into the wall of the house by following the manufacturer's instructions for drilling the hole through your wall and mounting your RV plug securely.

Your tiny house on wheels is now ready for the source of your power!

STEP 26: GENERATE SOLAR POWER, PART 1: UNDERSTAND HOW IT WORKS

This step can be skipped for those of you living solely on-grid, as it will cover everything surrounding generating off-grid solar power. There are options for generating power in other methods, such as wind power, but solar energy is the most universal and practical method for generating power off-grid.

Generally speaking, solar and off-grid power is a vast topic. In fact, many books exist specifically on the subject. We will scratch the surface and cover the overarching steps but will not get deep into the weeds of generating solar power. You should use these steps to guide you, but supplement your installation with more in-depth solar-specific installation guides elsewhere.

The system we are building is standard, and energy flows as follows: light from the sun hits the solar panels providing DC power, that current flows through a breaker and into a charge controller, which flows to a battery where it is stored. The DC then flows to an inverter which converts it to AC. This AC then flows into the tiny house subpanel, where it is dispersed to your various circuits (see Diagram 14).

Diagram 14

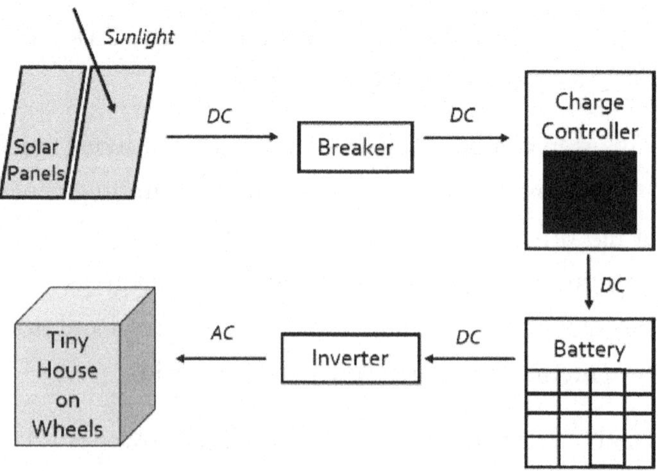

A note about generating electricity: think of this as an investment with a clear return. Installing off-grid electricity is not cheap. It can easily cost you between $10,000 and $20,000 upfront, though a significant tax credit can effectively cut that cost in half in some countries. There are ways to make it cheaper than $10,000 with some creativity and time but think of this as the price range.

Before you write this off as too expensive, think about the amount of money you will save in the long run, never having to spend a dime on electricity again. If you are spending $100 on your electricity each month now, that is $12,000 over the next ten years. If you were to spend a reasonable $15,000 up-front and receive a $7,500 tax credit, you would break even in about six years. Not too bad, considering there is no actual bill to pay.

There is also the massive environmental benefit of generating electricity that is 100% clean, rather than the typical 30% (at best) of on-grid electricity.

STEP 27: GENERATE SOLAR POWER, PART 2: DETERMINE POWER NEEDS & COMPONENTS

Before even discussing the solar panels themselves, the first step here is to calculate the load of the tiny house. This calculation is achieved by choosing your appliances and calculating the power needs of each, which amounts to taking the appliance's power rating in Watts and multiplying it by the hours per day that the appliance runs. The result is a Watt-hour. For example, if you plan to have a television with a power rating of 80 Watts, and you watch television about two hours per day, you need 160 Watt-hours.

Take the total of all of your various appliances' power needs in Watt-hours, then multiply it by 1.3 to account for the energy lost in the system. This number will tell you the total power needed in the tiny house. A standard amount of energy needed for someone living full-time in a tiny house on wheels is about 4000 Watts--or 4 Kilowatts--per day.

Given this ballpark power demand of 4 Kilowatts per day, we now need to determine the solar panels that can support our demand. A typical solar panel will provide roughly 0.3 KW per day, which means a tiny house typically needs around twelve to fifteen solar panels to be completely off-grid. A tiny house on wheels has space for about two panels on the roof, and the weight itself is not desirable. This means that to power your tiny house on wheels with entirely off-grid power, you will need to mount solar panels separate from the house.

Before any mounting can occur, choose your solar panels. The solar panel type should be based on your latitude because this dictates your relationship with the sun. You should select your solar panels such that they will charge your batteries fully during one 24-hour period—more on the batteries in a minute.

As far as the panels, there are two main types to choose from: monocrystalline and polycrystalline. Monocrystalline is more efficient but more expensive. Each panel is rated between 120 and 400 kilowatts. Typically, a panel in the 250-300 kilowatt range will suffice.

Take your energy demand that you calculated already, and divide it by the kilowatt rating of the panels. The number remaining is the number of panels you need.

Next, it is time to choose a battery. Solar panels generate DC load, so the panels cannot charge the house directly, as the house is AC. Thus, the solar panels must first charge a battery. First, determine the voltage of the system, either 12, 24, or 48 Volts. The higher the voltage, the more efficient the system, but with more efficiency comes more upfront expense. As far as the type of battery itself, choose a solar battery that is a deep-cycle lead-acid battery. This allows for partial and deep slow discharges, which suit the needs of a tiny house on wheels.

Now that the general system is configured, select your charge controller. The charge controller regulates the voltage and current from the panels before the current goes to the battery. It prevents overcharging. You will want to use Max Power Point Tracking (MPPT) or Pulse Width Modulation (PWM). MPPT is more expensive but more effective and best used when operating under 113 degrees Fahrenheit (45 degrees Celsius) as the cell temperature. PWM is cheaper but less effective and best used when operating above 113 degrees Fahrenheit (45 degrees Celsius). Note that the cell temperature varies by the type of panel and is not the same as the ambient temperature. It is the temperature on the panel's surface, usually much hotter than the outside air. Whether you choose MPPT or PWM, you must choose a charge controller that matches the charge rating of your system, whether that is 12V, 24V, or 48V.

Next, select your inverter, which converts DC to AC. Like the charge controller, you need to match the system voltage requirements of 12V, 24V, or 48V. It also needs to match the maximum load of the system at any given moment, plus some margin for error. Be sure to take into account the starting power of appliances when determining this load requirement.

Inverters come in many forms, but the most common, if not the best option, is the pure sine wave inverter.

The modified sine wave inverter and square wave inverter both pose potential problems in that they don't work with all appliances.

STEP 28: GENERATE SOLAR POWER, PART 3: WIRE AND ASSEMBLE

It is now time to wire the batteries and the panels. The battery configuration must match the system voltage and total wattage, which you calculated earlier. This is best achieved by selecting 6 or 12 Volt batteries, which also have an Amp-hour rating, and then wiring them in series-parallel. Series wiring is when the positive terminal of one battery is connected to the negative terminal of the next. In contrast, parallel wiring is the connection of positive to positive and negative to negative terminals. Two of the same batteries connected in series will have double the voltage of each individual battery, but the amp-hours will remain the same. Two batteries connected in parallel are the opposite; they will have double the amp-hours, but the voltage will stay the same. Series-parallel combines both of these types of connections to reach the needed voltage and the needed amperage.

In designing your batteries, remember that the ultimate goal is to reach your Watt-hour need while matching your system voltage requirements. Furthermore, given the basic calculation: Watts = Volts x Amps, we also know that Watt-hours = Volts x Amp-hours. We already know our voltage needed (12, 24, or 48 V) and we know our Watt-hours needed from our earlier calculation. If we use the equation, dividing the total Watt-hours by the voltage will give us the number of Amps needed. This total amperage divided by the battery's Amp-hour rating will provide us with the number of batteries that need to be wired in parallel. The voltage of the system divided by the voltage of the battery will give us the number of batteries that need to be wired in series.

As an example, a 24 Volt system is wired in series-parallel. Eight batteries are each 6 Volt batteries, and they each have a rating of 370 Amp-hours. The first four batteries are wired in series, as are the second four batteries. These two sub-systems are wired in parallel with each other. Given the nature of these wiring methods, the parallel wiring amounts to 370 Amp-hours multiplied by 2 batteries, giving us a total of 740 Amp-hours. Likewise, the series wiring amounts to 6 Volts multiplied by 4 batteries, giving us a total of 24 Volts. This system would support a total Watt-hour load of 24 times 740 which is 17,760 Watt-hours. Remember that this system is purely an example; you should be methodical and intentional when designing your battery system.

Once the batteries are wired properly, it is time to select your solar cable. While always balancing cost, you should seek to find the option with the least resistance. As electrical current flows from the panels to the batteries, resistance causes a loss of energy, resulting in less electricity stored in the batteries. Resistance is related to the metal itself, so you should ideally choose copper over aluminum since copper is less resistant. Resistance is also related to the length and cross-sectional area of the cable—the longer and thinner the cable, the more resistance. To find the proper gauge of solar cable, use an online calculator like the Renogy online calculator. You will need to input the solar panel operating voltage and current, both of which are defined by the manufacturer of the panels and are typically found on the panel specification sheet. You will also need to input the length of the cable between the solar panel and battery. Lastly, you will need to input the expected loss percentage, which is around 3% for well-designed solar arrays.

The calculator will then spit out a number as an AWG, which stands for American Wire Gauge and is the standard measurement for solar cables. This number is the cable size that you need. When purchasing your cable, make sure that the voltage grade of the cable matches the maximum system voltage of the solar panel.

It is now time to select the inverter battery cables, which are important for both safety and efficiency. The wrong battery cable can lead to not supporting loads properly and overheating. To find a suitable cable, you will need to do your research. It is dependent on many factors, and there are many approaches found online. Factors to be considered include the current, voltage, length, thickness, rating, composition, and material.

STEP 29: GENERATE SOLAR POWER, PART 4: MOUNT THE SOLAR PANELS

The next part may seem like a big one, but it is pretty simple. It is time to mount the panels themselves. To mount the panel, we first need to choose the panel. There are various options, each with its pros and cons. As covered previously, the desirable option of mounting panels on the roof is simply not practical since it adds a lot of weight to the trailer. More importantly, it doesn't come close to providing the necessary amount of energy. Another option is the pole mount, where the solar panel is mounted upward in the air on a pole. A more expensive option that collects the most energy is the solar-tracker mount. These come in both active and passive forms, where the panel is moving with the sun to capture the most possible sunlight at any given moment. The final option, and the most practical one, is the fixed mount. The fixed mount option is simply the mounting of your panels on the ground in a stationary position, such that they capture the most energy possible given your location. It is simple and easy to maintain relative to other options. For those living in regions far from the equator, you can add a little more efficiency--about 4-5%--if you make your mount adjustable so that it can be at a sharper angle in the winter and a flatter angle in the summer. Whether this added efficiency is worth the added expense and hassle of an adjustable mount is a matter of preference.

The placement of the solar panels is important. It should be in a place that is always exposed to the sun while still being close to the tiny house to reduce the solar cable's resistance and make the installation simpler. As far as the build of the panel mounts, plan to tilt the angle of the solar panels based on your location. A basic google search will give you results for the optimal angle you should use. Sketch your mounts before building.

Now that you know the placement, tilt, and design of your mounts, build the structures out of wood. This build is a simple exercise of using 2x4s and should be a breeze after having already framed your house in Chapter 2. Be sure to plan for future changes with your mounts. If you move, you will need to make sure your solar setup can come with you. For this reason, as well as ease and environmental benefits, it is recommended that you use wood instead of cement as the foundation of these mounts. The panels are pretty heavy, so unless you are in an extraordinarily windy place, there is no need to cement the mounts to the ground. Follow manufacturer instructions regarding attaching the panels, but make sure that you plan ahead so that any built-in holes in the backs of the panels will line up with your mount. Lastly, you will need to ground your panels as we did with the tiny house.

Diagram 15

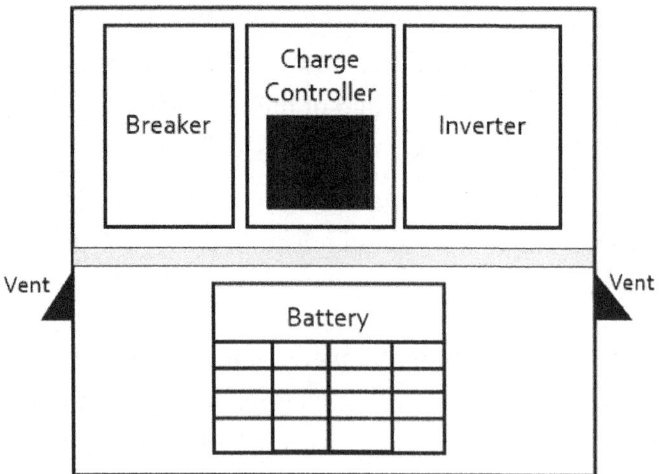

At this point, we have selected everything and mounted our panels. Now, it is time to assemble the various components safely. To build this assembly, build or buy an outdoor cabinet (see Diagram 15). This cabinet will have a top and bottom compartment that are separate from each other. The bottom compartment stores the batteries and has vents in the sides, as the batteries give off fumes that can damage the other equipment and cause a safety hazard. The breaker panel, charge controller, battery, and inverter are all connected and wired in the same order in the top compartment. Depending on your system, you will have several considerations, but always be sure to do the following:

- Cover the panels while installing and wiring so that no voltage is transmitted to your breaker panel. Ideally, this is disconnected entirely during installation.
- Make sure you follow manufacturer instructions for the installation of your parts.
- Make sure that your charge controller and inverter have built-in fuses for protection. If they do not, you will need to buy fuses that will satisfy this safety need.
- Make sure you are grounding the components correctly.
- Hire an electrician to check your work, always!

Once you have installed everything listed above, wire it and connect it to the subpanel in your tiny house on wheels. At this point in the build, you have effectively installed electricity!

STEP 30: INSTALL PROPANE FOR BACKUP POWER

The harsh reality of living off-grid is that you will almost always need a reliable backup source of power. Unfortunately, relying entirely on the sun for energy is quite risky and often simply not enough. If your solar array isn't getting enough sunlight, which can happen quite frequently in the winter, you will still need to be able to live your life. There are options for solar backup, as well as others like hydrogen and diesel, but the majority of the tiny house community uses propane. Using propane is much less desired than using renewable energy from an environmental perspective, but the reality is that technology and cost limitations currently make propane the top candidate for tiny house backup power. It also may serve as the primary source of power for certain appliances such as your kitchen stove or heater, which we will cover shortly.

The good news here is that while propane is a fossil fuel, it is highly efficient and relatively clean, much more than most other non-renewable sources. These characteristics are why propane has been dubbed a "green fuel" by some. Additionally, propane serves tiny house residents because it is affordable, portable, easily storable, and flexible. This flexibility means that propane often fuels stoves, propane water heaters, refrigerators, clothes dryers, and space heaters. Any time there is a new demand in your tiny house, a quick solution will likely involve propane while you save up and prepare for a longer-term solution that depends on renewable electricity.

As far as the use of propane for backup power, it's best to understand how this system works before diving into selecting the generator and installing it. Backup power is not as difficult as it may seem to the layperson. It is the addition of a second source of electricity that you can automatically or manually turn on via a switch.

The components of your backup power are an extension of the electrical system. It consists of the generator itself, running on propane, as well as a transfer switch. The transfer switch is a box that you install that directs the electricity from the subpanel and the generator into the house, allowing you to transfer between the two sources. There is the option of making the transfer an on-demand transfer, where the backup generator is automatically turned on based on the amount of electricity coming from the subpanel. This option is undoubtedly the most convenient, but it is ultimately very expensive, ranging well over $10,000. For this reason, it is recommended that you use a manual transfer switch, which is a switch next to your subpanel that you flip when you notice the power is out. Within a manual transfer switch, you can choose which circuits should run on the generator and which should not, so you have complete control over how electricity flows.

Regarding the generator itself, it is important to figure out what you will need to power in an outage and buy the properly sized portable generator. Typically, the 2-4 kW range is the output a tiny house will need, but it is best to calculate your needs, as previously mentioned when discussing the electrical demand of your tiny house on wheels. It is also important to account for elevation because propane efficiency decreases about 3% for every 1000 feet (300 meters) above sea level. Lastly, make sure your generator has a built-in inverter for functionality and safety purposes, as you need the current that flows into the house to be AC.

The installation of the generator setup is quite simple, but as always, prioritize the safety of yourself and others. The generator is portable, so all you need to do is plug it in when you need it to run. The transfer switch is a small box that you mount next to the electrical subpanel. You should follow the manufacturer's instructions when installing the switch, but essentially you will do the following: mount the transfer switch, wire the subpanel to the switch, and wire the electrical line from the generator to the switch. Choose the circuits you want to run when the transfer switch is on by flipping them within the transfer switch unit. Your backup power is ready.

Additionally, you should build an enclosure for the portable generator. Generators can be pretty loud, so an enclosure will reduce the noise significantly. Many people build an enclosure out of cinder blocks or similarly sound-proof materials. Do not make the enclosure completely sealed, as this poses a significant safety risk because energy and heat are being produced with nowhere to escape.

STEP 31: HAVE YOUR ELECTRICAL WORK CHECKED BY A PROFESSIONAL

Once the installation is complete, have an electrician check your work. This requirement cannot be stressed enough, and you are probably tired of hearing it repeated, but that is intentional. Spending a few hundred dollars to make sure that you can live your new life safely and with peace of mind is a no-brainer. You will not regret this critical step.

At this point, you have successfully installed your electricity, one of the most daunting and challenging parts of the build. Congratulations!

STEP 32: INSTALL PROPANE APPLIANCES

Propane appliances are different from the propane generator for backup power, so while they both use the same fuel, consider them different systems entirely. Propane appliances are fueled by propane, which is stored in a tank that sits outside of the tiny house on wheels. When you open the valve to the propane tank, the fuel will flow out of the tank, through a regulator, into the tiny house through a hole in the wall via a copper pipe, and continue to the various appliances via copper pipes. It is important to use a regulator because it makes sure that the propane is flowing steadily, thus reducing safety hazards.

As far as installing the propane lines, you will use similar methods as those used to install the plumbing, which will be covered in the next chapter. However, while the next chapter will cover the installation of PEX, which is a plastic pipe for water, propane requires copper plumbing. Working with copper plumbing is inherently more complex and can be risky from a safety perspective. A bad fitting results in propane leaks, which can be very dangerous if ignited or inhaled. For these reasons, it is recommended that you have a plumber do the work or check the work once you complete it yourself.

To install these appliances and the propane fuel system, do the math. Based on the appliances you have and how much you use them, you can quickly estimate the demand of your propane tank and plan accordingly. For many people who only use propane to fuel the stovetop, a small propane tank like the one used for a barbecue grill is perfectly sufficient. For those more heavily dependent on propane, larger tanks are available. Ultimately, the size of the tank is important but changeable in the future. The larger the tank, the less frequent the refills, but the heavier and more difficult to replace with a full tank.

In designing the propane fuel system, keep it simple. Design your tiny house such that the appliances are close to each other and the propane tank itself. The compact design reduces both complexity and weight.

Once designed, you are ready to install. Place your tank outside and attach the regulator to it according to the manufacturer's instructions. Then, drill the hole in your wall for the fuel line to enter. The hole should not be much bigger than the fuel line, nor should it squeeze the fuel line. Some choose to run this fuel line through the subfloor instead, depending on the design. Feed the pipe through the hole, but be careful not to bend the copper pipe too much, as an overbent pipe causes a leakage hazard. Continue to feed the line through the walls to the appliances. You will most likely need to find copper pipe fittings at your local hardware store to direct the propane flow properly.

Next, attach the pipes to the appliances. This can be done in a multitude of ways and will depend on the appliance and its fixtures. One example is flaring the pipe using a pipe flaring tool to secure the pipe to the nipple on the appliance. Another is using Teflon tape and a threaded fixture.

Once everything is installed, test all of your connections by putting soapy water on each connection. Open the tank and check each connection for bubbles. If the water bubbles, that means that propane is leaking. Turn off the tank and fix the connection, then test again.

Lastly, fill the hole around the pipe with spray foam so that it is properly insulated.

Your propane fuel is ready for use!

In this chapter, you learned a lot about electricity and energy in general. From understanding the basics of electricity to rouging in the wiring, to capturing solar energy, to backing up and fueling the tiny house with propane, you should now have a much firmer grasp on what it takes to get power for your tiny house on wheels.

To recap, electricity installation starts at the point where electricity is needed. Rough-in the wires and install the electrical boxes, and be sure to consider plumbing and map your installation. Then, install your subpanel, and consider outsourcing this part of the build. Install an RV-plug as the source for your energy. In the event that you are using solar power, make sure that all system components match in voltage, and make sure you properly consider demand, location, and energy loss when designing your system. Finally, install backup power and then have all of your electrical work checked by a professional.

You should now have a better sense of what you can do yourself and what you should hire a professional to do. Completing the installation of your electricity and propane systems is one of the most exciting pieces of the build because it is when your structure starts to become a livable home. When you turn on that light for the first time, you will feel the rush of your new life becoming an ever-closer reality.

5

HOW TO INSTALL WATER & WASTE SYSTEMS

Water and waste are often considered the second most intimidating part of a tiny house build, behind the electricity. Luckily, plumbing is much simpler than many first-time builders think.

While it has a few different components, plumbing ultimately is a matter of getting clean water in and getting dirty water and human waste out. We will consider these three different systems in a tiny house build: clean water, greywater, and blackwater. Clean water is the water that goes into the house, fed by traditional utilities, an on-grid spigot, rainwater, a well, or manually brought in. It is the water we drink, use to cook, use to wash our hands, and use to shower. Greywater is dirty water that is not contaminated with human waste, so it is the water that drains from the shower and sinks. Blackwater is the system that handles human waste.

STEP 33: DETERMINE YOUR WATER AND WASTE SYSTEM CONFIGURATION

While your tiny house on wheels may be on-grid full-time, it may be better to assume that the tiny house will be off-grid at some point. For the full-time on-grid tiny house, the greywater and blackwater systems can be connected, as the water will exit through a water utility line, just as it does in an RV or a permanent residence. You may also choose to use a septic system.

For the off-grid tiny house on wheels, the de facto option for a blackwater system is a composting toilet. In this setup, the blackwater system is fully isolated from the greywater and clean water systems. A composting toilet looks like a toilet, but it functions without running water. Instead, it has two compartments that capture and handle the two kinds of human waste. Urine is captured in a container that can be dumped easily, while fecal matter is captured in a built-in composting bin which turns it into compost. While it sounds a little bit different from your typical toilet, the composting toilet is a favorite among tiny house owners because it is very clean, doesn't smell, is great for the environment, and saves on costly water bills typically associated with flushing toilets. The compost toilet is highly recommended to all tiny house on wheels builders!

As far as the clean water and greywater systems, consider them two halves of a single system. Water flows into the house, and a portion is diverted to a hot water heater. Hot and cold water are both routed to faucets at sinks, the shower, and any appliances that need water, like dishwashers and laundry units. It is then drained into the greywater system and exits the house.

In determining this design, there are a couple of decisions to make. The first is to decide how you will source water. You can source water the old-fashioned way: dumping water into tanks by hand. This method is pretty simple and a good option for people building a tiny house on wheels that is not a permanent residence. Otherwise, the options include sourcing on-grid via traditional water utilities or an RV hookup. It can also be sourced off-grid from rainwater or a well. Some tiny house builders have even diverted water from a creek. Be sure to understand the local laws regarding water collection in general. Regardless, be sure to have the option for on-grid water even if you don't plan to hook up the tiny house on wheels (see Diagram 16).

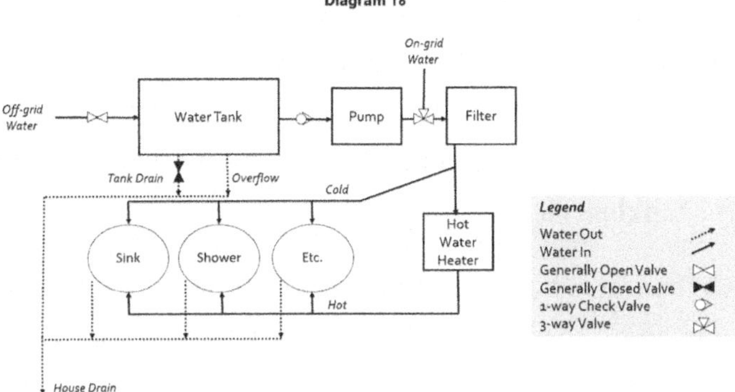

The second consideration is to figure out if and how you want to heat water. Water can be heated in a tank or in a tankless manner. Most opt for the tankless water heater because it is much lighter and a simple apparatus the size of a large pillow. Tankless water heaters can be powered via electricity or fuel. The electric option is much cheaper at the outset but does require electricity which may be limited off-grid. They are also easy to install and don't risk gas leaks, so they tend to be preferred. Another option is to use a propane or natural gas heater. These are a bit more expensive at the onset, but they are efficient and reliable, meaning a potentially longer-term financial benefit. The environmental impact is a downside, as is the complexity of installation. Lastly, consider alternatives like the wood-fired heater and the solar heater. Wood-fired heaters are convenient and simple but require you to wait for the water to heat up when showering, which is enough of a reason to avoid the wood-fired heater for most. The solar heater is the most environmentally friendly choice, but it is very expensive, sits outside, and takes up space. Considering these options, the most often recommended tiny house water heater is a tankless electric water heater.

As the water flows from the water heater to faucets and appliances, cold water flows directly from the water tank to faucets and appliances. The combined hot and cold water then flows down the drains and into the greywater system. These components are pretty standard, so the final decision is to determine how greywater will safely return to the environment. If you have access, you can return it to a sewer or dispose of it using the water hookup. You could also collect it and dump it elsewhere. For a more eco-conscious method, you can disperse your water back into the wetland by storing water and using it to water your garden. You could also use a branched drain system, which is just a hose that branches off in different directions, dumping the water out in a way that doesn't impact the land. A surge tank is another option, where you collect water in a drum or barrel and let gravity slowly push the water out of the bottom of the tank. It is important to understand your local greywater regulations before choosing your system and make sure that your method of disposing or recycling water does not damage the ecosystem in which you reside.

STEP 34: DETERMINE YOUR PLUMBING SYSTEM COMPONENTS

Now that you know how you are sourcing water, heating water, and disposing of water, you are ready to design your plumbing system. Note that this does not include the blackwater system, which we will cover later in the chapter as a separate topic. In your design, there are a few considerations to make. First and foremost, keep it simple and compact. Any appliances or drains should be close together and should all connect to one drain line. Also, make sure that the water system itself is accessible in the event you need to repair it or replace anything. Plumbing should always be below the electrical wiring. As far as the various components of the system, make sure you select your water tank, pump, filter, water heater, RV water inlet, PEX tubing, and sink and shower fixtures before beginning installation.

We will get more into the sourcing of rainwater in a bit, but make sure you install an RV water inlet to connect to a spigot. Furthermore, consider insulation in this inlet design if you live in a colder climate. You don't want frozen lines. The other option--if you know for a fact that your tiny house on wheels is staying in one place--is to connect your system directly to a well or on-grid water source.

Regarding the water tank that sits inside the tiny house as your holding tank for water, keep in mind that water is extremely heavy. You should use an RV tank of no more than 50 gallons (189 liters), which equates to over 300 pounds (136 kilograms) of weight. It is important to position the tank in a central place so that weight is not unevenly distributed side to side or front to back. Ideally, the tank goes above one of the axles. Make sure your tank has a built-in vent; if it does not, install a vent into it so that the tank pressure remains constant as water is pumped into and out of it.

As far as the pump goes, you need to move water through the system somehow. You may choose either a foot pump or a 12-volt pump, depending on your needs. A 12-volt pump is more work to install and an added piece of equipment that can malfunction, but ultimately more convenient. A foot pump is much simpler but requires you to do work when you want water. For a permanent residence, a motorized pump is preferred.

Next is the filter. You have a few different options for the filter. For one, you can install a filter like Diagram 16 shows, where the filter handles the water of the entire house at once. These are dependable and durable but a little bit more expensive than other kinds of filters. There is also something to be said for filtering water before processing it through the rest of your water system. The other option is to filter later down the line, at the point that the water exits. These filters are sink filters and shower filters, and they are much cheaper at first but ultimately cost you in maintenance and part replacement later. As far as the types of filters, there is the reverse osmosis filter, the gravity filter, the carbon filter, and several others. The type of filter depends on the water coming into your tiny house, your budget, and your ultimate needs, so do your research on water filters before selecting.

As we follow the flow of the water, the water leaving a filter for the whole house is then diverted. In one direction, the cold water goes directly to the shower, appliances, and sinks. Choose your appliances here with care and choose your shower and sink with functionality and space optimization in mind. We will get more into sinks and showers later in this chapter. In the other direction, water will flow to a water heater. While you can use a traditional tank to heat water, the more apparent choice is the tankless water heater. The tankless water heater runs cold water over hot coils as it passes to the shower, sink, and appliances, so it doesn't needlessly burn energy heating water in a tank. It can use electricity or propane, and ultimately doesn't cost an outrageous amount of money--some only cost a couple hundred dollars.

The last piece to the components of your tiny house water system is the plumbing itself. Copper is often considered a traditional method for cabin building. Still, the reality is that copper is not only harder to work with, but it is also less environmentally friendly to manufacture. The better option is PEX, a plastic material used by amateur and professional plumbers everywhere, specifically for water inflow. It is affordable and relatively easy to install. Aside from the PEX, you need a shutoff valve for the entire water system of the trailer, a 1-way check valve to ensure water doesn't flow back into the water tank, a valve to control whether you are feeding the system via a utility line or the off-grid source, and drainage pipes for your greywater. Options for outflow include metals and plastics, but metals are generally heavier and unnecessarily tricky. As far as plastics, the best options are PVC and ABS. PVC pipes are known for being inexpensive and easily identified from a measurement perspective, but also are a bit challenging to manage since pipes can not be unjoined, and glued pipes may leak if not done correctly. ABS is stronger than PVC and works well in the cold, though it may warp or deform at certain temperatures and sometimes fails to meet building code.

At this point, you now have the configuration and the components designed. It is just a matter of installing them! In the following few steps, we will cover one of the correct methods to install your plumbing: marking the inflow and drainage points as well as sink, shower, and appliances, followed by installing the shower, sink, and appliances to the point of completion, then installing the PEX and drainage pipes. Afterward, we will move onto the rainwater collection system and the blackwater system.

STEP 35: MARK THE KEY POINTS OF THE WATER SYSTEM

Before you just start putting PEX on the walls, there are many steps to be taken. First, design your overall layout of the water flow. Identify and mark the point where water will drain out of the tiny house, and avoid floor joists. Also, consider any premade drain holes in shower stalls, as these can force your drain to be in a particular location. Identify and mark the tank and pump area, as well as the shower, sink, laundry, and any other appliances that use water. Essentially, use your diagram from the previous two steps to mark the layout of the plumbing.

STEP 36: INSTALL THE SHOWER

There are various options for the shower. In all cases, the shower consists of a few key components. The visible components are the showerhead, the temperature valve, and the drain hole. The invisible components are the drain and the mixing valve, which combines your hot and cold water. One option is to create a custom-built shower. For building your shower custom, be sure to keep weight in mind. Most people think of a tiled bathroom when thinking about a shower, but the reality is that tile is often too heavy and can crack during transportation of the tiny house. For this reason, custom-built showers should focus on utility before aesthetics. One kind of custom-built shower is the wet bath, a popular type of bathroom in some parts of Europe among standard homes. It essentially makes the entire bathroom one big shower, such that nothing separates the water from the toilet and sink. The wet bath saves space and can save weight as well, and is a worthy option to explore if you are willing to put in the time to design it and make sure that it is properly sealed and ventilated. In all cases, the custom option is like anything else DIY: it costs less but requires more time, work, and care.

The final option, and the one that we will explore here, is the shower stall. This is a premade shower that you can install with relative ease into your tiny house. A shower stall kit only costs a few hundred dollars and can be quite small while still looking good.

Diagram 17

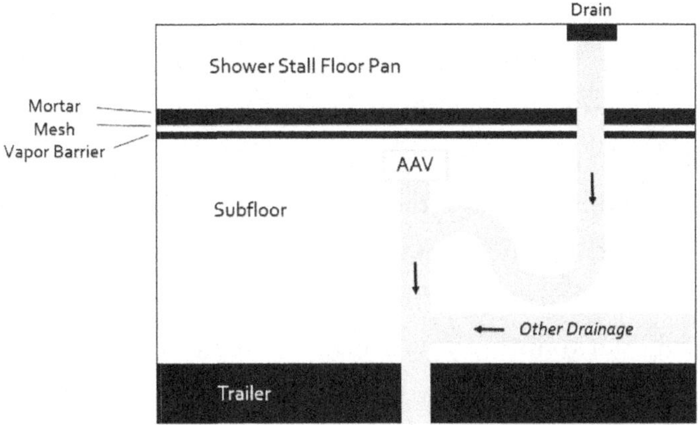

Once you have selected your shower stall, it is time to install it (see Diagram 17). Start by installing the mixing valve 40-44 inches (101-112 centimeters) off the ground by fastening it to the studs. When we run PEX, the hot and cold lines will connect to the mixing valve. Make sure it is level and follow manufacturer instructions. Next, install the faucet on the shower-head. You do not need to install the showerhead yet, as the faucet still needs to fit through the hole in the shower stall. Install any PEX plumbing that the shower stall will block. Use red PEX for hot water and blue PEX for cold water. The red and blue PEX are the exact same material, but the color helps identify the purpose of each line. You should also consider installing the insulation for the bathroom now, even though we will be covering that in the next chapter.

Now that the clean water plumbing is installed in the bathroom, it is time to install the greywater plumbing. This means installing the drainage system for the shower. Firstly, make sure you have room to install your drain. Your drain will include a P-trap or HepvO valve to prevent noxious gases from wafting into your tiny house through the drain. Most drainage systems are installed such that the main drain of the house runs beneath the subfloor, so you will have to pull up the subfloor to install your PVC or ABS pipe. If you do not have enough room, you can elevate your shower stall by using some 2x4 or 2x6 boards, placed on their thin edge around the rim of the shower enclosure. This gives you four to six inches of extra space for drainage and may also provide a nice finished look.

In this particular build, all of the greywater will leave the house underneath the shower, so it is time to install that hole. First, drill a pilot hole through the subfloor and trailer to ensure that your drain can escape the tiny house without interfering with an axle or joist. Once you have confirmed that your hole placement is correct, use a hole saw to drill a hole that will snuggly fit your PVC or ABS pipe, probably about 3.5 inches (9 centimeters) in diameter. Install the drain and P-trap or HepvO valve and PVC/ABS tee so that greywater from sinks and appliances can connect to the drain. Additionally, attach an air admittance valve to the drain line. The air admittance valve is a one-way valve that is activated by pressure changes, which keeps the drain free of clogs. Without a way to vent the line, you risk the water not flowing correctly. Similar to how a water bottle with a narrow opening glugs water when turned upside down, a ventless drain will not smoothly free the line of water, which is risky to the integrity of the plumbing system.

At this point, the shower stall installation can begin. First, install a moisture barrier using tar paper or similar material that you can find at a local hardware store. This barrier will protect the tiny house subfloor from wetness. Next, lay a steel mesh layer over the moisture barrier, and then apply mortar or floor mud according to manufacturer instructions. Make sure the mortar is level. The mortar acts as an adhesive once the shower stall is in place. Refer to Diagram 17 for a visual.

Next, install the shower stall, level the shower floor pan, and allow the mortar to set. Finish the drain by installing the drain cover. Finish the installation of the faucets and showerhead, and you are all finished!

STEP 37: INSTALL THE SINKS

The sink installation is a bit simpler than the shower. It is recommended that you purchase the sinks that you want first, then buy the proper greywater drainage to accommodate your sink connection type, since this can vary. In either case, the kitchen sink will have a similar setup to that of the shower. It consists of clean water coming into the sink connection, which may have a built-in mixing valve, as well as a drain and a P-trap or HepvO valve. Like the shower, include an air admittance valve. Your sink will likely require partial installation now, followed by completion once the kitchen countertop is installed. We will assume that the tiny house sink is being installed all at once in this build, but use your discretion when building. There is no one right way to build a tiny house, and there is no one right way to install a sink.

The order may vary depending on your sink type, but the steps to take include installing the drain basket using putty, so it is securely in place. Consider using a drain wrench to tighten the basket, then remove excess putty. This method ensures a waterproof seal. For a more industrial-style sink that is exposed, you may not need putty. Install the faucets and sink connection according to the manufacturer. Like with the shower, make sure all of the insulation and PEX are installed before installing the sink itself. Make sure this is accessible for maintenance. Once your countertops are installed, put a bead of silicone around the edge of the sink enclosure, then use sink clips to secure and tighten the sink to the countertop. Lastly, make sure all of the supply lines and drainage are connected properly.

STEP 38: INSTALL THE APPLIANCES THAT USE WATER

Now that you have installed the shower and the sink, you will have become pretty good at installing fixtures like this, so apply what you have learned to the appliances that use water, such as a dishwasher or laundry machine. Consider finding simple appliances that don't require hot water if at all possible. While an appliance like a laundry machine might have the ability to use hot water, you can always simply not attach a hot water line to the unit and instead only have cold water as an option for the appliance. This approach simplifies the plumbing system, reduces the demand for the water heater, and reduces the environmental impact of heating water. As with any appliance, be sure to follow the manufacturer's instructions and account for the same elements considered during the sink and shower installations: water barriers, insulation, PEX inflow, PVC or ABS outflow, line venting, P-traps/HepvO valves, and accessibility.

STEP 39: COMPLETE THE DRAINAGE

Now that you have installed your appliances, you need to connect all of them to the drain. That can begin with PEX or drainage, but drainage is a little bit more straightforward, even though it requires pulling up the floor. With each drain, your initial assembly of P-trap and air admittance valve is already in place. Now it is just a matter of connecting them. A common mistake in plumbing is to ignore the slope of the drain. Because water flows through the drain, gravity is our friend. For pipes in a tiny house, a general rule of thumb is a minimum drop of .25 inches for every horizontal foot (2 centimeters for every horizontal meter). Your drains definitely need to be sloped at least one-eighth of an inch per horizontal foot (1 centimeter per horizontal meter). Applying this math to your drain, install the remainder of your PVC or ABS pipe, and you will be finished with the drains. With that said, make sure your tiny house is level when installing all of your plumbing. If it is not level, water may not move properly. Next, reinstall any insulation in your floors, and reattach the subfloor. Lastly, make sure that there is a drain line and overflow line from your holding tank. The drain line should have a valve on it so you can completely drain the tank if you need. The overflow line, which does not have a valve, ensures the tank doesn't accidentally flood the tiny house.

STEP 40: INSTALL THE PEX PLUMBING AND COMPLETE THE REST OF THE SYSTEM

The next step is PEX plumbing, which is the inflow of water. This should be installed with the same slope as the drainage: one-quarter inch of vertical drop for every horizontal foot (2 centimeters per meter). The PEX plumbing should be below your electrical rough-in. Apply the same methods used to rough-in the electrical when running the water lines through the studs. Be sure to use red PEX for hot water and blue PEX for cold water. Also, be sure to take pictures of your build and measure and mark the placement of the tubing, which will help you locate the PEX one your wall is complete. This step is important, as it ensures that you don't accidentally puncture a line in the future. In this process, you will need to get acquainted with PEX itself. You can use a few helpful PEX tools, but PEX is ultimately an easy-to-use material. Just be sure not to overbend it, and you will be in good shape. One way to ensure this is to use PEX bend supports, which restrict the bend based on the diameter of the line. Also, make clean cuts and deburr your PEX when attaching it to fittings to ensure a clean and sealed fit.

As part of this installation, you also need to install the other system components, including the water tank, pump, filter, and valves. Refer to Diagram 16 as mentioned earlier to get a visualization, but ultimately the configuration should be simple, compact, and accessible. System maintenance is not an unlikely need in the future.

Ultimately, plumbing is a manageable and affordable endeavor, but it does require planning and adequately configuring your system. Keep in mind the weight of water, the importance of simplicity, and the fundamentals of plumbing, and your tiny house will be appropriately plumbed. Of course, if in doubt, hire a plumber to check your work.

STEP 41: DESIGN YOUR RAINWATER COLLECTION SYSTEM

There are many different ways to collect water, both on and off-grid, but one of the most popular and straightforward methods is the rainwater collection system. Consider this the alternative to your on-grid hookup, which you will certainly have if you are mobile and should have just in case, regardless of where your tiny house sits. The option we will explore is the rainwater catchment from the roof, so this system will collect rain as it runs off the roof by diverting it into an outdoor tank, then pumping it into the tiny house tank inside (see Diagram 18).

Diagram 18

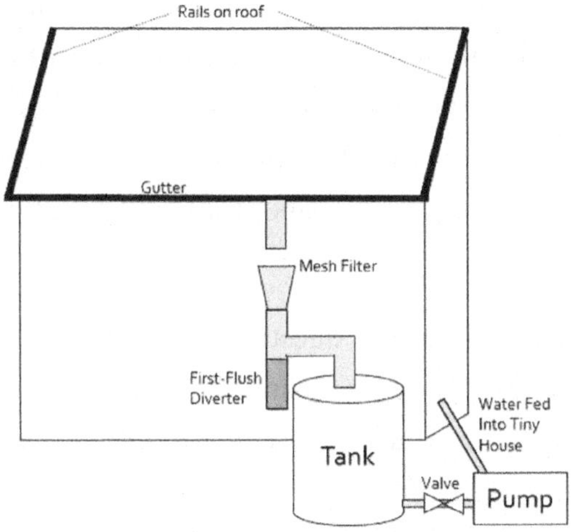

The first step is to plan out your system, and with many plans, you must first understand the laws. There are legal restrictions on water collection by country and state, so do your research before designing. Likewise, make sure that rainwater in your area is safe and abundant enough to collect in the first place. Once this initial research is finished, you need to answer two key questions: (1) how much water do I need? And (2) how much water can I capture from my roof?

To answer the first question, start by adjusting your expectations. The average US household consumes over 100 gallons (378 liters) of water in a day. You will need to cut that down significantly. This reduction is not particularly difficult, but it does take some adjusting. It becomes a simple matter of not wasting water. With that said, it can be beneficial to estimate your water consumption needs both now and in the future by writing down how you use water, then researching the amount of water that this requires. For example, a ten-minute shower uses about 20 gallons (76 liters) of water.

To answer the second question, we can apply a simple formula, both for those using the imperial system and those using the metric system. In either case, determine the area of the roof, either in square feet or square meters. This measurement is not the same as the area of the roof's surface, which is at an angle. Instead, this is the cross-sectional area, as though you are looking down onto the roof from directly overhead. By calculating this area, you are effectively determining how much area is available for water to hit your roof when it rains. Next, look up the rainfall depth in inches or millimeters, which tells you how much it rains where you live in a given period. With those two numbers, apply the following formulas, expressed first in the imperial system and then in the metric system:

- Area of roof (square feet) [x] Rain depth (inches/year) [x] .623 = Gallons Harvested

- Area of roof (square meters) [x] Rain depth (mm/year) = Liters Harvested

You now have the volume of water that you can harvest over a year. You can divide that number by 365 to understand the average rainwater harvest in a day. If this number is not sufficient, you will need to find an alternative source of water, which can be additional rainwater catchments that are not on the roof, a well, or an on-grid source.

STEP 42: INSTALL YOUR RAINWATER CATCHMENT SYSTEM

At this point, you can begin assembling and installing the catchment system. First, install gutters and rails on the side of the roof. The rails funnel the water into the gutter, so no rainwater is lost off the sides. Be sure not to extend the rails above the top of the tiny house, unless you have room to spare in the 13.5-foot (4.1-meter) height limitation of tiny houses on wheels. For the gutters, follow manufacturer instructions for installation, but also be sure to install a gutter protector. This feature will prevent debris from clogging the gutters and polluting the drinking water.

Next, position your storage tank. Make sure you use a tank gauge so you know how much water is actually in the tank at any given point in time. Use PVC pipes to move the water from the drain to the storage tank. The PVC will have a few components that help remove or filter debris. The first is the mesh filter, through which water vertically falls from the gutter into the mouth of the PVC collection. The filter prevents animals, leaves, and other grime from getting into the drinking supply. Beneath the mesh filter, your second line of defense is the first-flush diverter. The first-flush diverter is intended to rid the water of grime that comes off of the roof when it begins to rain. Within the professional rainwater collection community, there is a debate surrounding first-flush diverters. Some assert that while they work in theory, they don't adequately serve the intended purpose, causing more problems than they are worth such as maintenance issues or sediment buildup within the system.

The water will then flow to the catchment tank, so install your PVC to dump into the tank and make sure that the tank is sealed where it meets the PVC. Install a valve at the bottom of the tank, followed by an outdoor pump. This pump moves the water into the holding tank inside the tiny house on wheels, where it is then pumped through the filter in the house. For those seeking more sanitization of the water, consider installing a commercial purifier in the line as well. While filters and purifiers both rid the water of protozoa and bacteria, purifiers also rid the water of viruses.

Lastly, if not yet installed, be sure to install the RV water hookup to the side of the house and connect it to the pipes. Install a three-way control valve at the point of connection between the on-grid line and the off-grid line, as this will ensure that water is coming from one source or the other.

STEP 43: INSTALL YOUR BLACKWATER SYSTEM

The blackwater system seems intimidating at first, but in reality, it is quite simple. It is completely isolated from the rest of the plumbing system if using the composting toilet, which is highly recommended. There is the option to have septic or a blackwater holding tank, but that will not be covered here, as it is not the common design of tiny houses on wheels. Instead, we will explore the composting toilet because it is widespread due to its nature; it is environmentally friendly, clean, simple to maintain, does not smell, and costs between $500 and $1000. You can also build one yourself.

The composting toilet works as follows: urine is stored in one container, and solid waste is stored in another. The container for urine is simply removed and dumped, while the container for feces is a small composting unit, so it is turned into soil using organic materials that are easily added to the composting toilet.

As far as installation, simply secure it to the floor and follow the manufacturer's instructions. The composting toilet comes with a vent that pulls air through the composting chamber, which is very important because oxygen is needed to facilitate the composting process properly. Composting toilets are then emptied every two to four days.

That is all there is to it.

At this point, you have successfully installed your plumbing and water systems. You have learned the intricacies of clean water, greywater, and blackwater. You have learned how to install a rainwater collection system, and you have learned the fundamentals of plumbing. These topics are typically intimidating, but with the proper care, you can affordably make your tiny house that much more livable with running water.

We are nearing the point of livability in our build. The roof is over our head, the lights are on, and a hot shower is running. All that we have left is controlling the air and finishing the interior. The most complex parts are now behind us!

6

HOW TO INSTALL INSULATION, CONTROL THE AIR, AND FINISH THE WALLS AND CEILING

Air control is a crucial topic that is too often taken for granted. Most people have spent their lives living in homes that they did not build themselves, so they don't see the amount of thought that goes into insulation and temperature control. This chapter breaks down the topics you need to know and gives you a step-by-step guide to controlling air.

STEP 44: UNDERSTAND THAT AIR CONTROL IS MORE THAN JUST TEMPERATURE

Controlling the air is a multi-dimensional topic. The most obvious form of air control that we are all used to is air conditioning. This is absolutely a part of the air control topic, but it is not everything.

Altogether, there are four goals we are trying to achieve. The first is sealing the tiny house, which prevents air from leaking into and out of the house. The second is insulating the tiny house, which prevents the outside temperature from drastically shifting the inside temperature. The third is air quality control, which regulates humidity and pollution levels in the air. The fourth is air conditioning and heating, which controls the inside temperature. These four goals will be addressed throughout the remainder of this chapter.

STEP 45: SEAL YOUR TINY HOUSE ON WHEELS

An often overlooked step, sealing the tiny house is essential. People often assume that insulation is all that is needed, but insulation is only so valuable if air leaks through the tiny house seams. The construction of the house will be a critical component in sealing, which is one of the reasons the earlier chapters were so adamant about the importance of leveling and squaring your subfloor, walls, and roof.

To seal the house, you need to determine where there are drafts. There are different ways to identify drafts, but the best way to do this is a blower door test, which is a way of depressurizing the tiny house using the exhaust fans in your house, and then lighting an incense stick around the critical seams: doors, windows, exterior penetrations, intersections of wall and roof or floor and wall, and electrical outlets. In the event of a leak, use expanding spray foam to seal the junction.

STEP 46: DETERMINE AND INSTALL YOUR INSULATION

Insulation is highly dependent on location, so you need to plan for where you live and where you might live. Countries and states have codes that dictate what degree of insulation is necessary for a given climate. This insulation measurement is known as the R-value. The higher the R-value, the stronger the insulation, meaning less heat is transferred across the insulation. Determine the R-value you need based on your research into your location before even considering the type of insulation you need. Also, take a look at the needed R-value for your roof and subfloor, as these are higher than the R-value of the walls.

Given your estimated R-value, you can now select the type of insulation that best suits you, which comes down to factors like cost, ease of installation, and suitability to your climate. From a cost perspective, think about the cost to buy it and install it if a professional is required, but also consider the savings that come with better insulation. As far as climate goes, you need to be aware of how water condenses. When warm air hits a cold surface, it condenses into liquid water. Moisture that forms but cannot escape is a recipe for mold and rot. For this reason, you will need a vapor barrier, which is a plastic sheet that is impermeable to water vapor. The placement of the vapor barrier is very much dependent upon your climate. The vapor barrier should go on the side of the wall that is warmer, so for colder climates the vapor barrier is inside of the insulation and wall. In contrast, in warmer climates the vapor barrier is on the outside of the wall. Note that house wrap is a moisture barrier that lets vapor pass through, so moisture can escape through the house wrap but not through the vapor barrier. This combination of vapor barrier and house wrap protects your insulation and structure from moisture while also allowing any moisture that forms in the wall to escape.

For those living in variable climates, like many of you reading this book, the insulation and vapor barrier topic can be challenging to manage, but there are options. First, weigh your risk. Is it a higher likelihood of extreme heat or extreme cold? If there is a clear answer, you may act as though your climate is hot or cold. For those in a genuinely variable climate, you can install an aluminum barrier within the wall to serve as insulation while also properly purging occasional dampness. Alternatively, and probably most often recommended, is to use an insulation that is *also* a vapor barrier, most notably, spray foam.

There are many different types of insulation, each with its pros and cons:

- ***Rock wool or Roxul***: This option is a highly recommended option among DIY builders, as it is resistant to fire and sound, while also being rigid and easy to work with. It is not a vapor barrier, but it is water-resistant in case water comes into contact with it. The main downside is that it is a bit more expensive than other types of insulation, but not to the point of unaffordability.
- ***Closed-cell spray foam:*** Closed-cell spray foam (don't even bother with open-cell) is a vapor barrier, air barrier, and strong insulator, great for variable climates. Some builders swear by spray foam as the hands-down best option due to this unique trifecta. The downside is that it requires professional installation and can be expensive, while also being less environmentally friendly.
- ***Rigid foam board:*** This is an excellent option for the subfloor, as it has strong insulation capabilities and prevents moisture buildup. It is

easy to work with and can be installed on your own. The downside is that the R-value can vary and that there are fewer benefits compared to Roxul.

- ***Expanded polystyrene foam (EPS):*** This foam is another decent option. It handles water quite well, and it is a decent cost for the R-value. A downside is that bugs may like to live in it, and its environmental impact. Avoid its XPS counterpart, as that doesn't handle water well.
- ***Denim:*** The material that makes your jeans can be an insulator. People like the natural element of this and the fact that it can be sourced from recycled products, but it absorbs moisture which is a big negative.
- ***Wool:*** While this comes in two forms, stick to the wool batts instead of loose-fill, as it is more practical for tiny house insulation. It handles moisture well, and it is at least somewhat sustainable, even though it requires chemical treatment for preventing fire and insect infestation. The reality is that while it is a good option on paper, it is not as performant as Roxul or spray foam.
- ***Fiberglass batts:*** If you've ever been in an unfinished attic or basement, you've likely seen the pink and itchy fiberglass insulation. It is a pain to install and irritating to the touch during

installation, but it is a traditional option. It can be pretty bulky and a poor insulator, but it is relatively simple to install.

Once you have selected your insulation, purchase and install it. The installation will depend largely on the type you select, but it is not super difficult unless opting for spray foam, which simply requires a professional.

For the roof insulation, consider a combination of insulation to fit your needs. Generally, the R-value and moisture prevention of the roof must be prioritized. A rule of thumb is that the roof should have double the R-value as the walls.

STEP 47: INSULATE THE WHEEL WELLS

The wheel wells can be an Achilles heel in the design of a tiny house. If you aren't thoughtful, they can be a thermal bridge, the cold or hot metal of the wheel well altering the interior temperature. There are different approaches to manage this, one of which is boxing it and filling it with Roxul. Instead, we will explore a clever and proven method of boxing with foam.

Create a box out of cabinet-maker birch plywood, ½-inch (1-centimeter) thick. This box looks good and functions properly. Install foam board insulation leftover from the subfloor installation onto the inside of the box, prior to installation. If you do not have any, purchase a foam board that is the same R-value as the walls. Next, attach cleats to the floor and wall using glue and then nails. These cleats create tight pieces of wood to which you can attach your box. Attach the box to the cleats, and your wheel well is insulated and looks good on the eye as well (see Diagram 19).

Diagram 19

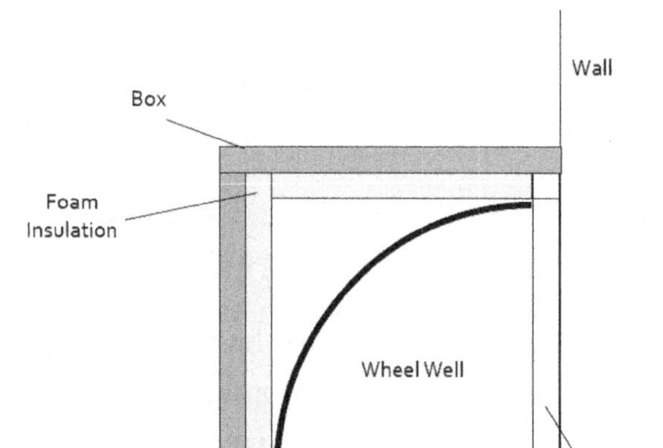

STEP 48: INSTALL THE VAPOR BARRIERS

We have already discussed this topic quite a bit, but in this sample build, vapor barriers should be installed after the insulation. That assumes a temperate or cold climate. You may have already installed yours at this point if you live in a warmer place, or if you opted for the insulation and vapor barrier hybrid that is spray foam. Ultimately, the vapor barrier is highly dependent on the climate of your home, and you need to research the topic for your given area. That said, most vapor barriers will be a plastic sheet of some kind, which will be fixed to the walls. Check out the IBC and IRC codes to understand which zone you are in and the vapor barrier demands of that zone, select your vapor barrier, and install according to the manufacturer's instructions. Be sure not to skip the vapor barrier as it is vital to the long-term health of your tiny house on wheels.

STEP 49: FINISH YOUR TINY HOUSE WALLS & CEILING

Once vapor barriers are in place, it is time to finish the walls and ceiling of your beautiful tiny house on wheels. First, choose your wall finish. Don't use something heavy like drywall; instead, use plywood or tongue and groove paneling. Choose this based on weight, rigidity, and the aesthetic that you are seeking.

Level your trailer again. Start at the bottom of your wall if you are using tongue and groove panels. Complete from bottom to top, one wall at a time. Nail the panel into the stud at the tongue, which will be covered by the groove of the next panel. Stagger the vertical seams of the panels for an appealing look, and cut around electrical boxes by setting the board, marking it, and cutting it with a jigsaw. Paint or stain the walls to your liking.

For the ceiling, follow the same process, but paint or stain the panels first, as it is difficult to do overhead.

That is it! At this point, your walls and ceiling are finally finished.

STEP 50: INSTALL PASSIVE AIR VENTS AND EXHAUST VENTILATION

Now that the walls are finished, you can deal with ventilation. Air vents are important in controlling the flow of air into and out of tiny houses, keeping the air clean and free of noxious gasses, the main being carbon dioxide, which shouldn't exceed 1000 parts per million (PPM). While some tiny house builders simply opt for windows as the air quality control measure, this option has its shortcomings since it is not purpose-built to handle air, and it requires the air quality outside to be better than the air quality inside. For permanent residences, only using windows in a tiny house on wheels is not recommended. Instead, one should install both of the two primary forms of ventilation: exhaust and passive.

Most of us are familiar with exhaust vents as they are the vents that make up the range hood of a stovetop and the vents turned on during a shower. These vents are only on when the kitchen or shower is in use, allowing hot and humid air--as well as carbon dioxide and carbon monoxide--to escape the tiny house. In general, these vents will be no different than those of a traditional house. They are electrically powered and switched on when needed. Shower exhaust fans should be placed at the top of the shower, while range hoods should be placed at least 27 inches (69 centimeters) above the cooktop, though follow manufacturer instructions.

Passive air vents, on the other hand, are subtler. They are simply small holes in the sides of houses that allow for air to passively flow through the house at all times. Air comes in through one vent and escapes through another. Tiny house builders often place more than one pair of vents in the house, and put some high and some low, so that air is never trapped in a nook of the tiny house. Passive air vents can be purchased through your hardware store and are simple additions that make your house not only safer but fresher and more pleasant.

In all cases, the air vent will require a hole to be drilled through the wall. First, make a wooden block that will act as the external mount for your ventilation hole. Next, figure out where the vent goes. Check your framing, electric, and plumbing diagrams so as not to damage your other systems. Carefully cut away your siding so that the block can fit into a slot. You will probably need a handheld saw for this, like an angle grinder with a cutoff wheel. Once the block is set into the slot, screw the block into the frame of the tiny house, then use a long drill bit to bore a hole from the outside to the inside of the tiny house. Drill this hole at a slight upward angle, about 1 or 2 degrees, as this will use gravity to prevent water from getting trapped in the vent. Now use a hole saw to cut the hole to match the diameter of the vent you are installing. Some insulation materials, such as Roxul, will work well here, while others may be a bit more difficult to cut through. Finally, install the vent tube, attach the exterior component, and then install the interior vent apparatus following the manufacturer's instruction. Seal the outer seam of the block using foam to prevent any water from entering the cavity. You now have ventilation installed!

STEP 51: SELECT AND INSTALL HEATING AND COOLING SYSTEMS

Heating and cooling systems are pretty important when considering how to make your tiny house comfortable. Unless you live in a place like San Diego, you probably will need a way to heat your space, cool your space, or both. Like any other part of the build, planning for your needs now and in the future is key to choosing the right system.

As far as cooling systems go, the two popular options are a mini-split and a window unit. Mini-splits are typically the top choice because they are pretty easy to install on your own, they look good, and they don't take up window space, nor do they require any duct-work. They are also quite efficient, and perhaps best of all, they act as a heating system as well as a cooling system. Window units, on the other hand, are pretty self-explanatory, as they are the same as what you have likely seen your entire life. You need to buy one, install it into the window or wall, and plug it in. They are a bit cheaper than a mini-split, but they don't look very good, and they don't provide heating capabilities. Regardless of what you pick, follow the manufacturer's instructions when installing, and always be sure not to drill through anything important in your walls.

As for heating systems, there are several different options aside from the mini-split. The electric heater, either radiant or forced air, is simply purchased and plugged in, making it an easy and affordable option. However, it draws from your electric source, which could be considered good or bad depending on your situation and priorities. Between the two options, radiant electric heaters are quiet and slow to heat a space, while forced-air electric heaters are noisy and quick to heat a space.

The second option is the propane heater, which is a good option among the off-grid tiny house community. One of the main complaints is that it may not be sufficient in the winter and that it is a fossil fuel. That said, it is simple and cheap.

Another option is the wood stove. The wood stove is cozy and looks good. It also can be multipurpose, being used for cooking. The downsides to the wood stove are that it takes up space, can provide too much heat, and requires a bit of planning if not professional installation.

A couple of other options worth checking out are the heat pump and the floor heater. Heat pumps are an excellent option for chilly but not super cold climates, while floor heaters help keep tiny houses on wheels from being cold to the touch.

Altogether, consider your options and select a mini-split or combination of systems that work best for your needs.

STEP 52: CONSIDER FURTHER AIR QUALITY CONTROL MEASURES

Not to be forgotten, follow code, and don't leave air quality up to chance. You should install smoke detectors, carbon monoxide detectors, propane detectors, and radon detectors where applicable. Even when construction is done properly, air quality issues can arise.

On the topic of air quality and safety in general, consider having a fire extinguisher as well as an oxygen monitor.

In this section, you successfully handled the air control and the walls. You now have all of the major systems in place, and the rest is simple compared to what you have already achieved. Pat yourself on the back for having officially completed all of the systems of the tiny house on wheels. It is now time to make the house feel like a home.

7

HOW TO COMPLETE THE INTERIOR STRUCTURE: FLOOR, STAIRS, & STORAGE

Now comes the fun part! With the tough work behind us, the rest is pretty smooth. It is time to take off your house builder hat and put on your designer hat because now it is time to think all about how to utilize space best. There is still a small amount of building to be done, but it is simple. Mostly, we are now thinking about the utility of space, flow, and visual appeal. In this chapter, you will put the finishing touches on the build by handling the floor, building the stairs to the loft, and dealing with storage in the process.

STEP 53: STAIN THE SUBFLOOR OR INSTALL THE FLOOR

When it comes to flooring, there are many options, but before discussing types of flooring, it's best to think about what matters when picking your flooring. First of all, weight always must be considered. Some types of flooring are particularly heavy and unnecessarily load your axles. Avoid this. Secondly, consider durability. This includes not only the ability for the floor to withstand time and wear but also for it to withstand jostling and movement while on the road, which eliminates options like tile. Durability also must include water resistance. Like any other part of the tiny house on wheels, water is your nemesis. Next, think about how easy it is to install and maintain or clean over time. Of course, don't forget how the floor looks from a style perspective! Finally, consider the environmental impact and sustainability of the flooring that is sourced.

With these above options in mind, there are several choices for your tiny house on wheels, and it doesn't need to be one choice for the entire tiny house. You may choose to floor your loft with carpet, your bathroom with vinyl, and leave the rest as a finished subfloor, for example. Regardless of your configuration, let's cover the options:

- ***No flooring***: This is a fantastic option that many don't consider. No flooring means using the subfloor as the floor itself. Just stain the plywood, and you have a beautiful, lightweight, cheap, and easily maintained floor. The only issue can be a cold floor, but good insulation and a comfy rug in the living area can prevent and mitigate this.
- ***Vinyl:*** If you are going to go with flooring at all, vinyl is typically the best bet. It is durable, affordable, easy to work with and maintain, and has a lot of variety in visual style. Its major downside is that it is plastic and therefore not sustainable.
- ***Laminate***: Laminate shares many of the qualities of vinyl, but instead of plastic, it is usually made of particle board. While this sounds good because it is more natural, the reality is that laminate is easily damaged in humid environments, even when treated. Unless you are in an arid climate, laminate is not worth the risk.
- ***Carpet***: While carpeting your entire tiny house is probably not what most people consider nowadays, carpet can be an excellent choice for a bed area, loft, or hangout. It is insulating and cozy on the feet, but it is susceptible to stains and wears out quickly. Carpeting is also a bit

challenging to install for beginners. To avoid carpeting installation, many may choose area rugs instead.

- ***Hardwood***: Simply put, don't do it. Hardwood is very tempting because it looks gorgeous, but hardwood is tough to maintain, very challenging to install, pushes four figures in cost, and can be pretty heavy depending on the type.

Altogether, the flooring is a personal choice, but keep it simple. With the advancement in flooring technology, specifically vinyl, you don't need to get too cute with the flooring if you choose to install a floor at all.

Once you select your flooring, follow instructions by the manufacturer. For staining the subfloor, it is as simple as reading the instructions on the can of stain and then finishing with a polyurethane seal. For installing vinyl, it will be quite similar to the wall installation you already completed.

STEP 54: DESIGN AND BUILD THE STAIRS

Since you have a tiny house loft, you need to get to it. It is strongly recommended by the tiny house community that you avoid using a ladder. Ladders seem fun and adventurous at first and appear to save a lot of space.

The reality is that the fun wears off, they don't necessarily save space, and they present a legitimate safety concern.

Instead, opt for building stairs. They are safer and much easier to live with, especially if you are sleeping in your loft. Going to the bathroom at night will be way easier with stairs, and safety will be less of an issue. If you build the stairs with intention, they can act as a phenomenal storage cabinet.

That is why we are going to think about building a stair-shaped cabinet rather than a staircase.

Essentially, your staircase is an assembly of boxes customized to your needs. A quick google search will reveal hundreds of ideas for how to utilize the space.

But how do you actually design and construct it? It is quite simple. First, you need to plan out the space that the stairs will take up. This design comes in many forms (see Diagram 20). There is the total run, which is the total horizontal space of the entire staircase unit. There is the total rise, which is the total vertical space of the entire staircase unit, which is simply the height of the top of the loft floor to the main floor. There is also the rise and run of each step.

In a typical standard house, the rise and run of each step are 7 inches (18 centimeters) and 11 inches (28 centimeters), respectively. In a tiny house, one should follow code, but generally the rise and run can vary depending on need and preference. Your rise can be anywhere from 7-11 inches (18-28 centimeters), while your run can be 9-11 inches (23-28 centimeters).

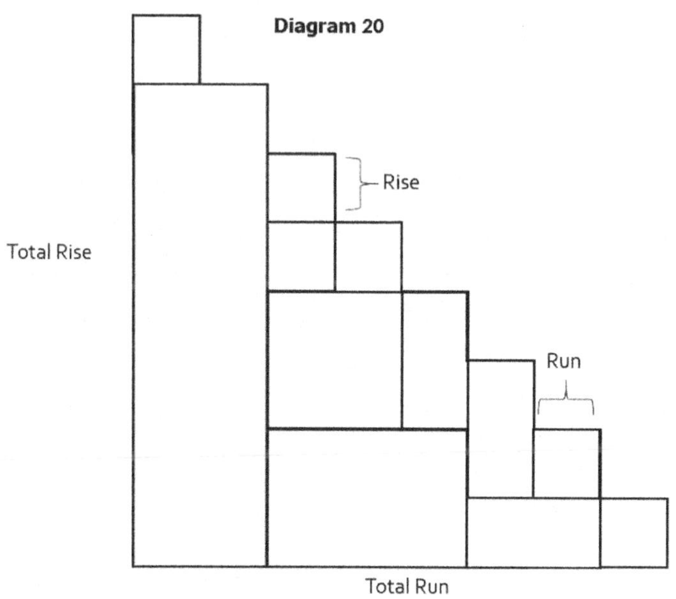

To determine the design you need, first determine the height of the floor to the loft, which is the total rise. Then, determine the desired rise of each step, somewhere between 7 and 11 inches (18 and 28 centimeters), though preferably closer to 7 inches (18 centimeters). Now determine the number of steps you need by dividing the total rise by the desired rise and rounding up to the nearest whole number.

For example, let's say your loft is 79 inches off the ground, and your desired rise is 8 inches. 79 divided by 8 equals 9.875. Round this up to 10, and you know that your staircase will need 10 steps. Next, take the 79 inches and divide it by 10 steps, which is equal to 7.9 inches in rise per step. You now know that you will have 10 steps each at 7.9 inches in rise.

Now that you know the rise of each step, the overall rise, and the number of steps, you can determine the total run. First, decide the run of each step. Next, take the number of steps and subtract one from that number. We subtract one because the top step is the loft itself, so it does not account for horizontal space but does account for vertical space. Multiply this number by the run of each step, and you now have your total run. Make sure that you have space for this in the tiny house!

To continue our example, let's say that the desired run is 9 inches. We know that there are 10 steps, so we take 10 and subtract 1 because the top step is the loft. This gives us 9 steps to account for horizontally. We then multiply 9 steps by the desired run of 9 inches, giving us 81 inches in total run.

You now have designed the overall size of your tiny house staircase.

Next, it is time to sketch out the configuration of the boxes that make up this staircase (see Diagram 20). The boxes are essentially cubbies that make up the staircase cabinet. The horizontal width of the box is a multiple of the run of a step, while the vertical height of a box is a multiple of the rise of a step. In our example, that means that each box can have a width of 9 inches, 18 inches, 27 inches, etc.; and that each box can have a height of 7.9 inches, 15.8 inches, 23.7 inches, etc.

When determining the boxes that you will make, don't just randomly decide what to have. Logically plan out the use of the storage space and design accordingly. For example, you may want to store coats or dresses in the cabinet space, in which case you need a tall cubby. Use images online to inspire you, but ultimately design the space for your specific storage needs.

Once you have determined the dimensions of all the boxes you need, it is time to build the modules or boxes themselves. Use half-inch plywood with a smooth finish, and secure using a standard butt joint, which simply means putting one end on top of the other. Since the boxes are load-bearing, the boxes must be built such that the sideboards are sandwiched between the top and bottom boards (see Diagram 21). Build using wood glue and wood screws, and make sure everything is square.

Diagram 21

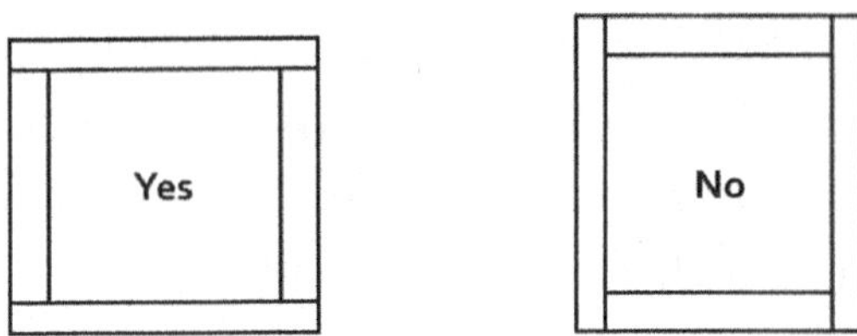

After the glue has dried, add a backboard to the boxes. Once all the boxes are finished, assemble them by screwing them together. Then screw the staircase unit to the wall by screwing directly into the studs.

Lastly, install a handrail along the wall according to code.

You have now successfully built a staircase and created massive storage space in a tiny home.

In this chapter, you have finally completed the interior structure and finish. You have a functioning house. All that's left is making it a home.

8

HOW TO FINISH THE INTERIOR: FURNITURE, KITCHEN, BATHROOM, APPLIANCES, & DECORATION

At this point, everything is going to be custom to the builder. There is no more construction or system installment left to be done. Any appliances or furniture that needs to be installed can be installed according to the manufacturer's instructions, and anything that is custom-built can be researched independently. Instead, consider this chapter the celebration of your ability to design the interior of your own tiny house. It is the home stretch, pun intended. Each step will simply give you an understanding of your options. The rest is up to you!

STEP 55: SELECT THE APPLIANCES

Before beginning to finish the tiny house on wheels, select your appliances. There is a whole litany of options, which are highly dependent on your needs. Don't assume that smaller appliances will be cheaper. In fact, it is quite the opposite in some cases since they are serving a more specific need. It is often best to seek appliances in the RV and boating industries, as these appliances are also designed for tight quarters. Overall, you must weigh which appliances you need and which appliances you simply want. Some common kitchen appliances include a refrigerator, a freezer, an oven, a toaster oven, a stove, a microwave, a pressure cooker, an electric kettle, and a coffee maker. Other than those already addressed earlier in the book, some common appliances outside of the kitchen are a clothes washer/dryer, fans, a dehumidifier, a vacuum cleaner, and clothing irons. Take a minimalist approach to your appliances by writing down how much you use each appliance today in your not-yet-tiny life. This exercise should give you a sense of what is a need versus just a space-wasting and energy-draining convenience.

STEP 56: INSTALL THE KITCHEN

Kitchens come in all shapes and sizes, even in a tiny house on wheels. This is a very personalized space, as it should suit your needs based on cooking preferences and frequency, appliances, and the number of people. As with the rest of your build, think long and hard about your needs before designing and building the kitchen.

As far as the cabinetry goes, you have three different options: build it yourself, buy small cabinets, or repurpose old cabinets that you have or that you acquire. Each has a different associated price and requires a different amount of work.

While there is no right way to finish the kitchen, you will typically start with the cabinets. Install the cabinet structures themselves. Then, before finishing the cabinetry, install major appliances like your dishwasher, fridge, oven and stove, or even a laundry machine if that is in your kitchen. Next, finish the cabinets by hanging the doors. Add the countertops, then finish the sink installation. Add smaller appliances and fixtures, and decorate. Your kitchen is ready for use.

STEP 57: FINISH THE BATHROOM

The bathroom too is quite personalized and has largely been installed, since we have already covered the installation of the compost toilet, shower, plumbing, unfinished sink, and ventilation. Now, it is just a matter of finishing the cabinetry and putting the finishing touches on the sink and shower if any are required. Depending on your build, now is the time to double-check that the bathroom is sufficiently prepared to handle moisture and water.

STEP 58: BUILD, BUY, AND SET UP THE FURNITURE

Furniture is an essential feature of the tiny house because it has many different purposes, ranging from functionality to visual appeal to secondary storage. The visual appeal aspect, as well as whether or not the furniture is comfortable, is somewhat self-explanatory. Don't buy a couch that doesn't feel good to sit on. That is just common sense. However, with a little bit of creativity, you can create incredible furniture that looks good, works well, and optimizes space.

For your bed, there are numerous options aside from simply plopping down a mattress on the loft. One is the murphy bed, which is a bed that retracts down from the wall. This option is a massive space saver and can have built-in storage or an attached couch to convert for both day and night use. Beds can also be convertibles from other pieces of furniture, such as a table or sofa. These kinds of furniture are fantastic because they allow you to use only what you need at any given point in time. Many DIY guides exist online for building these types of beds, and you can even pay someone to build one for you if you wish. Another sleeping option is to build your bed as a trundle underneath an elevated kitchen or your staircase. In this sense, the bed doesn't take up space during the daytime, only requiring space at night, making it a massive space saver if one is willing to spend the time designing and building it.

Tables are another place where creativity can save a ton of space. Instead of just placing a table near your kitchen area, you can instead hang a table from the wall so that it is only a table when it is in use. Likewise, tiny house builders have designed tables that slide out like a kitchen drawer, so the table is hidden away in the cabinetry when not in use. Lastly, and perhaps most simply, get a foldable table that you can store away when you don't need it.

As far as furniture goes in general, creativity is king. Nevertheless, there are options for you to purchase multi-purpose, modular, and compact furniture for affordable prices. Ikea is notorious for having small furniture that fits quite nicely in a tiny home.

Spend time planning and have fun with this process before you even begin your build, as the final design of the space is very much a factor in how the walls, floors, stairs, and loft are constructed.

STEP 59: DECORATE

Decoration is one of the most personalized elements of someone's home, but there are a few tricks that can help make the space really pop. Embrace lighter and more neutral colors, as these will truly make your tiny house feel bigger. Use plants to decorate, giving your area a more natural feel. Make patterns in your cabinetry instead of hanging heavy and spacious artwork. Perhaps most importantly, design with utility in mind! Most pieces of decoration should also be functional. One example is hanging your kitchen utensils beneath a shelf rather than storing them in a cabinet. Another example is to hang items like skis or a mountain bike on the wall as art. It looks good, and it gives an important belonging a proper home. These kinds of examples go on and on, and can easily be researched by just looking at images of tiny houses online or spending the night living in one. Enjoy the creative process!

STEP 60: CELEBRATE & LIVE TINY!

You did it. You built a tiny house on wheels. Time to celebrate and enjoy your newfound freedom in your new life!

LEAVE A 1-CLICK REVIEW

I would be incredibly grateful if you would take just 60 seconds to leave a review of my book on Amazon, even if it's just a few sentences. Thank you!

Scan the QR code below to leave a review.

CONCLUSION

Through this guide, you have learned everything it takes to build a tiny house on wheels, from the first moment you start designing your house all the way to the decoration of the finished interior. Along the way, you should have gotten a holistic sense of what it takes to build, what you should and should not do, when you should outsource work, and ultimately why building a tiny house on wheels is beyond just creating a structure. It is a journey that will teach you a lot about concrete topics like construction and plumbing and solar energy, while also teaching you to have a much deeper connection with the process of building your own home. Ultimately, the goal for most is to build a new life, and the tiny house on wheels is the way to achieve that goal.

When it comes to construction and design, it is important not just to know the different pieces of the puzzle--the clean water system, the window installation, the subfloor, etc.--but to understand how those pieces fit together. While this book is likely not 100% of the information you need to build your specific tiny house, it should have gotten you significantly closer to achieving your goal. And more importantly, it should give you a sense of what you still need to learn more about, while helping you identify the blind spots you didn't see before. This book should have given you peace of mind and a much more thorough understanding of this specific form of construction, something that a layperson can do on their own.

I hope you feel empowered and better prepared to embark on this journey, and if you are in the midst of your tiny house build, that you're able to use this guide as a form of a checklist and a way to consider all the options holistically.

Once your house is built, you will have created something that you can and should be proud of. You will have taken a massive step toward a better life, one of more financial freedom and more meaning. One of adventure and connection to nature and the environment. Take the time to appreciate everything you have learned through the build and everything you have learned about your actual needs. Most importantly, take the time to celebrate a dream turned into a reality.

If you liked the book, please leave a review! And be sure to check out some of my other tiny house books as well. Thank you for reading!

OTHER BOOKS YOU'LL LOVE!

Scan the QR code to get the book!

Just For You!

A Free Gift To My Readers

This quickstarter is a gift to readers to apply what they learn in this book. Within this quickstarter are a task checklist, a budgeter, a location tracker, and a list of things not to do. Get yours now and make your tiny house dream a reality!

jordanliberata.com

RESOURCES

CHAPTER 1

E. (2017, November 15). *Tiny House Security: How to prevent a stolen tiny house*. The Tiny House. https://www.thetinyhouse.net/tiny-house-security/

Editors of Nolo. (2016, May 23). *Building a Tiny Home: Should I Put It on Wheels or on a Foundation?* Www.Nolo.Com. https://www.nolo.com/legal-encyclopedia/building-tiny-home-should-i-put-it-wheels-foundation.html#:%7E:text=The%20primary%20benefit%20of%20building,on%20wheels%20can%20be%20relocated.&text=Another%20benefit%20to%20building%20on,not%20legally%20considered%20a

Juras, M. (2020a, November 6). *Top 6 Easy-to-Use Programs to Design Your Own Tiny House*. Tiny House

Bloom. https://tinyhousebloom.com/top-6-tiny-house-design-software/

Juras, M. (2020b, November 6). *What is the Average Weight of a Tiny House on Wheels?* Tiny House Bloom. https://tinyhousebloom.com/average-weight-tiny-house-on-wheels/#Road_Limits

Juras, M. (2021, July 26). *The Best Lightweight Building Materials For a Tiny House*. Tiny House Bloom. https://tinyhousebloom.com/lightweight-building-materials/#:%7E:text=Light%20structural%20timber%20like%20fir,work%20well%20on%20the%20interior

Lisefski, A. (2020, April 17). *Tiny House Safety - 20 Tips From A Safety Expert*. The Tiny Project. https://tiny-project.com/tiny-house-safety-20-tips-from-a-safety-expert/

Max Size & Weight For A Tiny House On Wheels Without Permits. (2021, July 13). Super Tiny Homes. https://www.supertinyhomes.com/tiny-house-on-wheels-weight-guide/

Schultz, B., & Grotyohann, L. (2019, November 24). *seven principles*. Actually Tiny. https://actuallytiny.com/our-vision/

Ulmer, B. (2017, April 6). *The Top Ten Tools You Need to Build a Tiny House*. PADtinyhouses.Com. https://padtinyhouses.com/tools-to-build-a-tiny-house/

What Kind of Tools Are Needed to Build a Tiny House. (2013, January 1). [Forum Discussion]. Reddit. https://www.reddit.com/r/TinyHouses/comments/1v3wz5/what_kind_of_tools_are_needed_to_build_a_tiny/

White, A. (2016, June 4). *Tiny House Plans Quartz Model by Ana White* [Design Plans]. https://www.ana-white.com/sites/default/files/Tiny%20House%20Plans%20Quartz%20Model%20by%20Ana%20White%20-%20med%20res.pdf

CHAPTER 2

Bilodeau, M. (2020, March 14). *The Adventure of Subfloor Construction.* TinyHome.Io. https://www.tinyhome.io/subfloor/

Bushradical. (2020, December 9). *Simple off grid cabin (Part 2). . .. . .that anyone can build & afford* [Video]. YouTube. https://www.youtube.com/watch?v=k2ejcEddQt8

Clark, P. (2020, December 5). *Read This Before You Order a Metal Roof.* Tumbleweed Houses. https://www.tumbleweedhouses.com/read-this-before-you-order-a-metal-roof/

Isaiah Industries, Inc. (2016a, January 11). *Options.* Roofs for Tiny Homes. https://www.

tinyhouseroof.com/options/

Isaiah Industries, Inc. (2016b, January 11). *Options*. Roofs for Tiny Homes. https://www.tinyhouseroof.com/options/

Juras, M. (2019, November 25). *How to Build a Tiny House Subfloor On a Trailer*. Tiny House Bloom. https://tinyhousebloom.com/how-to-build-tiny-house-subfloor-on-trailer/

Juras, M. (2020a, February 18). *Innovative and Clever Tiny Home Bed Solutions*. Tiny House Bloom. https://tinyhousebloom.com/tiny-home-bed-solutions/

Juras, M. (2020b, October 21). *What is the Ideal Height for a Tiny House Loft?* Tiny House Bloom. https://tinyhousebloom.com/loft-height-ideal/#Building_a_Loft_Why_Every_Tiny_House_Needs_One

Juras, M. (2020c, October 21). *What is the Ideal Height for a Tiny House Loft?* Tiny House Bloom. https://tinyhousebloom.com/loft-height-ideal/#:%7E:text=To%20answer%20the%20question%2C%20there,tall%20as%203'6%E2%80%9D

Juras, M. (2020d, December 15). *Tiny House Framing 101: Everything You Need to Know to Frame Your Tiny House*. Tiny House Bloom. https://tinyhousebloom.com/tiny-house-framing/#:%7E:text=For%

20traditional%20and%20tiny%20houses,materials%20-for%20a%20hybrid%20construction

Juras, M. (2021, July 26). *Best Tiny House Roof Options: Complete Tiny House Roofing Guide*. Tiny House Bloom. https://tinyhousebloom.com/roof-options/

Land to House. (2015, February 11). *Tiny House 36 - Install Loft Floor* [Video]. YouTube. https://www.youtube.com/watch?v=WCXrCsxyYNY

Lisefski, A. (2020, May 6). *Advanced Framing For Tiny Houses*. The Tiny Project. https://tiny-project.com/advanced-framing-for-tiny-houses/

Lstiburek, J. (2010a, March 10). *BSI-030: Advanced Framing*. Building Science Corporation. https://www.buildingscience.com/documents/insights/bsi-030-advanced-framing

Lstiburek, J. (2010b, July 15). *BSI-001: The Perfect Wall*. Building Science Corporation. https://www.buildingscience.com/documents/insights/bsi-001-the-perfect-wall

M. (2020a, June 4). *Everything You Need To Know About Roofing Your Tiny House*. Tiny House for Us. https://tinyhousefor.us/tiny-houses/everything-you-need-to-know-about-roofing-your-tiny-house/

M. (2021, June 30). *The Ultimate Guide To Building A Tiny House*. Tiny House for Us. https://tinyhousefor.us/resources/the-ultimate-guide-on-building-a-tiny-house/

Mitchell, R. (2020a, April 29). *Framing My Tiny House*. The Tiny Life. https://thetinylife.com/framing-my-tiny-house/

Mitchell, R. (2020b, August 27). *Tiny House Dimensions: What Size Can A Tiny House Be Without Breaking The Law?* The Tiny Life. https://thetinylife.com/tiny-house-dimensions-what-size-can-a-tiny-house-be-without-breaking-the-law/

O. (2020b, December 15). *Tiny House Loft Plans | MyOutdoorPlans | Free Woodworking Plans and Projects, DIY Shed, Wooden Playhouse, Pergola, Bbq*. MyOutdoor-Plans | Free Woodworking Plans and Projects, DIY Shed, Wooden Playhouse, Pergola, Bbq | Step by Step DIY Articles about Free Woodworking Outdoor Plans, Starting with Wooden Furniture up to Pizza Ovens, Pergolas, Sheds, Doghouses and Barbeques. https://myoutdoorplans.com/shed/tiny-house-loft-plans/

O. (2020c, December 15). *Tiny House Roof Plans | MyOutdoorPlans | Free Woodworking Plans and Projects, DIY Shed, Wooden Playhouse, Pergola, Bbq*. MyOutdoor-Plans | Free Woodworking Plans and Projects, DIY Shed, Wooden Playhouse, Pergola, Bbq | Step by Step

DIY Articles about Free Woodworking Outdoor Plans, Starting with Wooden Furniture up to Pizza Ovens, Pergolas, Sheds, Doghouses and Barbeques. https://myoutdoorplans.com/shed/tiny-house-roof-plans-2/

Rookie Roost DIY. (2016, August 19). *Roof Rafters & Loft Joists // DIY Tiny House Build* [Video]. YouTube. https://www.youtube.com/watch?v=fcQTmZ0MarQ

Rubio, P. (2020, March 12). *How To Install Eave Trim For Metal Roofing. Step By Step Guide.* Western States Metal Roofing. https://www.westernstatesmetalroofing.com/blog/install-eave-trim-metal-roof

Skills Institute Press. (2014, October). *How to Build a Tiny House – Part 7: Building the Roof.* Grit. https://www.grit.com/community/tiny-house-building-the-roof-ze0z1410zcalt/

Sokol, E. (2019, August 8). *How to Install Drip Edge on Shed Roof.* Plasticine House. https://plasticinehouse.com/how-to-install-drip-edge-on-shed-roof/

Straight and Stable: The Ins and Outs of Tiny House Leveling. (2020, October 7). Tiny Home Builders. https://www.tinyhomebuilders.com/blog/tiny-house-leveling/

Tiny, A. (2019, December 13). *Leveling Your Tiny House Trailer Before You Build* [Video]. YouTube. https://www.

youtube.com/watch?v=WoZdshyZ824&feature=youtu.be

White, A. (2016, February 5). *How to Build Floor for Tiny House on Trailer: Ana White Tiny House Build [Episode 2]* [Video]. YouTube. https://www.youtube.com/watch?v=RE9Lg7FgGJM

White, A. [Ana White]. (2016a, February 12). *How to Build and Frame Tiny House Walls: Ana White Tiny House Build [Episode 3]* [Video]. YouTube. https://www.youtube.com/watch?v=K0ba7YRrITw&t=56s

White, A. [Ana White]. (2016b, February 19). *How to Build and Frame a Tiny House Roof: Ana White Tiny House Build [Episode 4]* [Video]. YouTube. https://www.youtube.com/watch?v=RAPrTYwWF40

White, A. [Ana White]. (2016c, March 11). *How to Install Metal Roofing on a Tiny Home: Ana White Tiny House Build [Episode 6]* [Video]. YouTube. https://www.youtube.com/watch?v=vIrRL_jFeK0

White, A. [Ana White]. (2016d, April 15). *How to Build a Loft Bed Triple Bunk Bedroom: Ana White Tiny House Build [Episode 11]* [Video]. YouTube. https://www.youtube.com/watch?v=q29yQlrPerM

CHAPTER 3

Builders, T. H. (n.d.). *Moisture 101: Mold Prevention for Your Tiny Home*. Tiny Home Builders. Retrieved September 9, 2021, from https://www.tinyhomebuilders.com/blog/moisture-101-keep-tiny-home-dry/

Door Rough Opening Sizes and Charts. (n.d.). EZ-Hang Door. Retrieved September 9, 2021, from https://ezhangdoor.com/door-rough-opening-sizes-and-charts/#:%7E:text=Framing%20rough%20opening%20sizes%20are,off%20of%20the%20sub%2Dfloor

Front Door Options for Tiny Houses That Look Amazing! (2020, June 1). Tiny House Giant Journey. https://tinyhousegiantjourney.com/2014/07/29/front-door/

HouseImprovements. (2012a, September 23). *How To Install An Exterior Door* [Video]. YouTube. https://www.youtube.com/watch?v=lKN5r91JAIA

HouseImprovements. (2012b, September 24). *How To Insulate A Window Or Door* [Video]. YouTube. https://www.youtube.com/watch?v=0T_vP2l8LOU&t=294s

HouseImprovements. (2014, February 14). *How To Install a Window with a Nailing Flange* [Video]. YouTube. https://www.youtube.com/watch?v=YttTTi-hNZc

Hubble, A. (2021, January 27). *The House Wrap Comparison Guide for 2019.* Barricade Building Products. https://barricadebp.com/news/the-house-wrap-comparison-guide-for-2019

Juras, M. (2020, November 8). *The Best Exterior Siding for Your Tiny House: Lightweight and Durable.* Tiny House Bloom. https://tinyhousebloom.com/best-exterior-siding/

M. (2021, June 30). *The Ultimate Guide To Building A Tiny House.* Tiny House for Us. https://tinyhousefor.us/resources/the-ultimate-guide-on-building-a-tiny-house/

Nelson Tiny Houses. (2017, September 21). *How to Install a Window in a Tiny House* [Video]. YouTube. https://www.youtube.com/watch?v=o14IE5ssJn4

Neri, S. (2017, June 2). *Front Doors of Tiny Homes: What You Need to Know.* Straight Line Design & Remodeling. https://straightlinedr.com/front-doors-tiny-homes-need-know/

Novotny, E. (n.d.). *Why Your Home Needs Siding.* Windows on Washington. Retrieved September 9, 2021, from https://www.windowsonwashington.net/blog-full/why-your-home-needs-siding#:%7E:text=Siding%20protects%20your%20house%20from,your%20home%20in%20the%20future

S. (2020, March 25). *Choose the right windows for your tiny house on wheels*. Fred's Tiny Houses and Trailers. https://fredstinyhouses.com.au/choosing-windows-for-your-tiny-house/

Spesard, J. (2020, December 5). *5 Window Considerations for Tiny House RVs*. Tumbleweed Houses. https://www.tumbleweedhouses.com/5-window-considerations-for-tiny-house-rvs/

White, A. [Ana White]. (2016a, March 18). *House Wrap Installation: Ana White Tiny House Build [Episode 7]* [Video]. YouTube. https://www.youtube.com/watch?v=b_QPE6TRwZk&t=161s

White, A. [Ana White]. (2016b, March 25). *How to Install Windows and Doors: Ana White Tiny House Build [Episode 8]* [Video]. YouTube. https://www.youtube.com/watch?v=mul_jkiDWgE&t=195s

White, A. [Ana White]. (2016d, June 3). *Tiny House Siding: Ana White Tiny House Build [Episode 17]* [Video]. YouTube. https://www.youtube.com/watch?v=iyuLjJcXPU4

CHAPTER 4

A. (2021, January 14). *How to Choose the Right Solar Wires and Cables for PV System*. Best Of Solar Energy. https://bestofsolarenergy.com/how-to-choose-the-right-solar-wires-and-cables-for-pv-system/

actually tiny. (2019a, July 15). *Sizing Electrical Service For A Tiny House* [Video]. YouTube. https://www.youtube.com/watch?v=sD97AIGvdxk&list=PL2mjT9zAY_sWIzsmD4bF_3_MlCbVLZrBG&index=3

actually tiny. (2019b, July 21). *Wiring a Tiny House Sub Panel* [Video]. YouTube. https://www.youtube.com/watch?v=SDDyBf0h1_s&list=PL2mjT9zAY_sWIzsmD4bF_3_MlCbVLZrBG&index=4

actually tiny. (2019c, August 12). *Tiny House Circuit Planning and Electrical Rough In* [Video]. YouTube. https://www.youtube.com/watch?v=2N-tzAD1Id8&list=PL2mjT9zAY_sWIzsmD4bF_3_MlCbVLZrBG&index=5

BigRentz, Inc. (2021, April 19). *The Ultimate Guide to Building a Generator Enclosure | BigRentz*. Big Rentz. https://www.bigrentz.com/blog/ultimate-guide-building-generator-enclosure

Davidson, J. (2021, June 27). *How To Install Solar Panels For Your Tiny House | Step-By-Step Guide*. Tiny Living Life. https://tinylivinglife.com/2019/06/how-to-install-solar-panels-for-your-tiny-house-step-by-step-guide/

Dinulescu, C. (2020, December 23). *Breaker Box Anatomy: How Do Electrical Panels Work?* Penna Electric. https://pennaelectric.com/electrician-blog/breaker-box-anatomy-how-do-electrical-panels-work/

DIY Off Grid Solar System. (n.d.). Instructables. Retrieved September 9, 2021, from https://www.instructables.com/DIY-OFF-GRID-SOLAR-SYSTEM/

Farneth, I. (2019, May 6). *How to choose the right solar wire size.* Renvu Solar. https://www.renvu.com/Learn/How-to-choose-the-right-solar-wire-size

Hometown Acres. (2021, January 17). *Budget Friendly Emergency Backup Power - Transfer Switch* [Video]. YouTube. https://www.youtube.com/watch?v=EiRW6rpLxyQ

Hosfeld, D. (2019, October 13). *Off Grid Electricity: What You Need to Know.* An Off Grid Life. https://www.anoffgridlife.com/off-grid-electricity-what-you-need-to-know/#:%7E:text=Off%20Grid%20Electricity%20Options&text=Solar%20(such%20as%20photo-voltaics)%20generally,the%20natural%20flow%20of%20water

How much would an electrician charge to do the electricity in a tinyhouse? (2017, May 14). [Subreddit]. Reddit. https://www.reddit.com/r/TinyHouses/comments/6b64ly/how_much_would_an_electrician_charge_to_do_the/

How to Install Ground Rods. (2021, June 8). In *wikiHow*. https://www.wikihow.com/Install-Ground-Rods

Jacobson, M. Z., & Jadhav, V. (2018). World estimates of PV optimal tilt angles and ratios of sunlight incident upon tilted and tracked PV panels relative to horizontal panels. *Solar Energy, 169*, 1–66. https://doi.org/10.1016/j.solener.2018.04.030

Johnson, J. (2020, February 27). *The Ultimate Guide to Off-Grid Generators*. Down to Earth Homesteaders. https://downtoearthhomesteaders.com/the-ultimate-guide-to-off-grid-generators/

Juras, M. (2019a, November 11). *5 Tiny House Appliances You Must Power with Propane*. Tiny House Bloom. https://tinyhousebloom.com/propane-appliances/

Juras, M. (2019b, November 11). *5 Tiny House Appliances You Must Power with Propane*. Tiny House Bloom. https://tinyhousebloom.com/propane-appliances/

Kreutzer, D. (2021, May 4). *Is It Safe To Plug My Camper in? How to Test a Shore Outlet*. Camper Report. https://camperreport.com/is-it-safe-to-plug-my-camper-in-how-to-test-a-shore-outlet/

Miah, S. (2021, January 6). *5 Best Generators for Tiny House (Updated For 2021)*. Globo Tools. https://globotools.com/best-generator-for-tiny-house/

Mitchell, R. (2021a, May 3). *Solar Panels For Tiny Houses: How I Went Off Grid With My Tiny House With Solar Power*. The Tiny Life. https://thetinylife.com/tiny-house-solar/

Mitchell, R. (2021b, May 3). *Why You Need To Be Using Propane In Your Tiny House*. The Tiny Life. https://thetinylife.com/tiny-house-propane/

Mitchell, R. (2021c, May 3). *Why You Need To Be Using Propane In Your Tiny House*. The Tiny Life. https://thetinylife.com/tiny-house-propane/

Mitchell, R. (2021d, August 9). *Tiny House Electrical Guide – Wiring & Powering Your Tiny Home*. The Tiny Life. https://thetinylife.com/tiny-house-electrical/

Mitchell, R. (2021e, August 9). *Tiny House Electrical Guide – Wiring & Powering Your Tiny Home*. The Tiny Life. https://thetinylife.com/tiny-house-electrical/

NFPA. (n.d.). *NFPA 70®: National Electrical Code®*. Retrieved September 9, 2021, from https://www.nfpa.org/codes-and-standards/all-codes-and-standards/list-of-codes-and-standards/detail?code=70

Off-Grid Power Systems for Tiny Houses. (2017a, September 3). The Off Grid Tiny House. http://theoffgridtinyhouse.com/off-grid-power-systems-for-tiny-houses

Off-Grid Power Systems for Tiny Houses. (2017b, September 3). The Off Grid Tiny House. http://theoffgridtinyhouse.com/off-grid-power-systems-for-tiny-houses

Optimum Tilt of Solar Panels. (2017, March 18). Solar Panel Tilt. https://www.solarpaneltilt.com/

Solar Cable Gauge Calculator. (n.d.). Renogy United States. Retrieved September 9, 2021, from https://www.renogy.com/calculators#tab_solar-cable

Stephens, A. (2019, November 11). *What is the Best Portable Generator for a Small Home and Travel Adventures? 8 Great Options*. Tiny House Expedition. https://tinyhouseexpedition.com/what-is-the-best-portable-generator-for-a-small-home-and-travel-adventures-8-great-options/

Storgaard, M. (2020, September 8). *Are RVs Grounded? Helpful Answers (For Beginners)*. Go Downsize. https://www.godownsize.com/are-rvs-grounded-facts/#:%7E:text=How%20do%20You%20Ground%20an,grounding%20pin%20has%20broken%20down

Taylor-Parker, P. (2020, January 8). *Generator Sizing Guide For Off-Grid Solar Systems*. Unbound Solar. https://unboundsolar.com/blog/generator-sizing-guide

The Tiny Life. (2020, October 20). *Tiny House Electrical - How to wire your tiny house* [Video]. YouTube. https://www.youtube.com/watch?v=bAOyC1odkw0&feature=youtu.be

Thiele, T. (2021a, April 16). *Why Electrical Grounding Is So Important*. The Spruce. https://www.thespruce.com/what-is-grounding-1152859#:%7E:text=What%20Is%20Electrical%20Grounding%3F,fault%20in%20the%20wiring%20system

Thiele, T. (2021b, August 5). *Amperage, Not Voltage, Poses the Greatest Danger With Electrical Shock*. The Spruce. https://www.thespruce.com/amperage-not-voltage-kills-1152476#:%7E:text=Voltage%20vs.,of%20the%20volume%20of%20electrons

This Old House. (2017, May 7). *How to Install a Manual Transfer Switch for a Portable Generator | Ask This Old House* [Video]. YouTube. https://www.youtube.com/watch?v=GLgtFCJlVFQ

Tiny Home Builders. (n.d.). *Face Your Fear: Tiny House Electrical Wiring*. Retrieved September 9, 2021, from https://www.tinyhomebuilders.com/blog/face-fear-tiny-house-electrical-wiring/

Tiny Nest. (2015, June 18). *Tiny House Propane Rough-In (Ep.33)* [Video]. YouTube. https://www.youtube.com/watch?v=xm2WPHTk06M

White, A. [Ana White]. (2016, April 1). *Electrical Planning and Installation: Ana White Tiny House Build [Episode 9]* [Video]. YouTube. https://www.youtube.com/watch?v=SvMRPrGhsK0

Wild Wonderful Off-Grid. (2018, December 28). *Electrical Panel Installation In OFF-GRID Cabin* [Video]. YouTube. https://www.youtube.com/watch?v=Hw9e3HW6XVU

Xaxx, J. (n.d.). *How to Install an LP Gas Line Through the Wall of a House*. Hunker. Retrieved September 8, 2021, from https://www.hunker.com/13408668/how-to-install-an-lp-gas-line-through-the-wall-of-a-house

CHAPTER 5

actually tiny. (2019a, May 26). *Tiny house plumbing overview* [Video]. YouTube. https://www.youtube.com/watch?v=c6J-zET3vHY

actually tiny. (2019b, December 10). *Tiny House Under-Sink Plumbing* [Video]. YouTube. https://www.youtube.com/watch?v=ucJrpeLL2tM

actually tiny. (2021, January 5). *Building Systems: Plumbing + Electrical* [Video]. YouTube. https://www.youtube.com/playlist?list=PL2mjT9zAY_sWIzsmD4bF_3_MlCbVLZrBG

Ana White. (2016, December 5). *Tiny House Plumbing System* [Video]. YouTube. https://www.youtube.com/watch?v=YZl5iefn9bQ

Bennett, M. (2020, January 7). *Water Options for Tiny Homes.* Hipster Real Estate. https://www.hipsterrealestate.net/home/2020/1/3/water-options-for-tiny-homes

Delsota, J. (2020, March 20). *A Definitive Guide To Creating A Rainwater Collection System For Your Tiny House.* Tiny House Life. https://tinyhouselife.org/a-definitive-guide-to-creating-a-rainwater-collection-system-for-your-tiny-house/

E. (2019a, October 14). *An Introduction to Grey Water in Your Tiny House.* The Tiny House. https://www.thetinyhouse.net/an-introduction-to-grey-water-in-your-tiny-house/

E. (2019b, October 14). *Tiny House Plumbing: Build your Bathroom, including Shower & Toilet.* The Tiny House. https://www.thetinyhouse.net/tiny-house-plumbing/

Handeeman. (2016, August 11). *MAKING A CUSTOM tiny SHOWER PAN* [Video]. YouTube. https://www.youtube.com/watch?v=BY6_LxauYT0

Home Depot. (2021, July 28). *How to Install a Direct to Stud Shower Enclosure* [Video]. Home Depot. https://www.homedepot.com/c/ah/how-to-install-a-direct-

to-stud-shower-
enclosure/9ba683603be9fa5395fab90883af5f6

Home RenovisionDIY. (2019, March 10). *The Ultimate Pex Shower Installation Video | A to Z* [Video]. YouTube. https://www.youtube.com/watch?v=fQhshM1XSWg

Home Repair Tutor. (2016, June 24). *How to Install PEX Pipe in Bathrooms (Quick Tips) -- by Home Repair Tutor* [Video]. YouTube. https://www.youtube.com/watch?v=FYS1TSzfVZY

Juras, M. (2019, December 22). *How to Set Up a Rainwater Catchment System for Your Tiny House*. Tiny House Bloom. https://tinyhousebloom.com/rainwater-catchment-system-setup/

Juras, M. (2021, July 26). *Best Practices For Easy Grey Water and Black Water Maintenance In Tiny Homes*. Tiny House Bloom. https://tinyhousebloom.com/grey-water-black-water-maintenance/

Kolloen, S. (2021, January 15). *Tiny House Bathrooms •*. Insteading. https://insteading.com/building/tiny-house-bathrooms/#shower

M. (2020, November 20). *Getting Creative with Your Tiny House Shower*. Tiny Heirloom. https://www.tinyheirloom.com/tiny-house-shower/

M. (2021, June 30). *How-To Guide: Choosing The Best Tiny House Water Heater*. Tiny House for Us. https://tinyhousefor.us/tiny-houses/how-to-guide-choosing-the-best-tiny-house-water-heater/

Maxwell-Gaines, C. (2020, July 27). *Rainwater Harvesting 101*. Innovative Water Solutions LLC. https://www.watercache.com/education/rainwater-harvesting-101

Mitchell, R. (2020a, April 28). *Designing Your Dream Tiny House Bathroom – Advice From A Full Time Tiny Houser*. The Tiny Life. https://thetinylife.com/designing-your-dream-tiny-house-bathroom-advice-from-a-full-time-tiny-houser/

Mitchell, R. (2020b, April 29). *How To Setup A Rainwater Catchment System*. The Tiny Life. https://thetinylife.com/how-to-setup-rainwater-catchment-system/

Mitchell, R. (2021a, May 17). *Tiny House Plumbing: A Simple DIY Guide Including Tanks, Diagrams, And Costs*. The Tiny Life. https://thetinylife.com/tiny-house-plumbing/

PEX Tools | PEX Tubing Tools at PexUniverse.com. (n.d.). PEX Universe. Retrieved September 9, 2021, from https://www.pexuniverse.com/pex-tools

R. (2018, February 11). *A Tiny House -Friendly Alternative to a P-Trap*. Small Around The World! https://

smallaroundtheworld.com/a-tiny-house-friendly-alternative-to-a-p-trap/

Tiny House Giant Journey. (2018, May 4). *Tiny House & RV Plumbing for DIYers* [Video]. YouTube. https://www.youtube.com/watch?v=loGKLy1gPmg&feature=youtu.be

Tiny House Listings. (2017, June 21). *THE BEST TINY HOUSE TOILET* [Video]. YouTube. https://www.youtube.com/watch?v=01GoBVH7_tE

To First Flush, or not to First Flush. (2021, March 27). BlueBarrel Rainwater. https://www.bluebarrelsystems.com/blog/first-flush-diverter/

Wallender, L. (2021, May 16). *5 Main Types of Plumbing Pipes Used in Homes.* The Spruce. https://www.thespruce.com/basic-types-of-plumbing-pipes-1822487

CHAPTER 6

actually tiny. (2019a, June 4). *How To Box In and Insulate Tiny House Wheel Wells* [Video]. YouTube. https://www.youtube.com/watch?v=wm0gLz4DXV0

actually tiny. (2019b, December 18). *Installing Passive Air Vents In A Tiny House* [Video]. YouTube. https://www.youtube.com/watch?v=8g812rXjQTI

Back, A. (2021, June 21). *Installing a Wood Stove in a Tiny Home*. Salamander Stoves. https://salamanderstoves.com/installing-a-wood-stove-in-a-tiny-home/

Carter, T. (2021, February 28). *House Wrap vs Vapor Barrier*. Ask the Builder. https://www.askthebuilder.com/house-wrap-vs-vapor-barrier/

Crandell, P.E., J. H. (2021, March 2). *2021 IBC & IRC Adopt Improved Vapor Retarder Requirements*. Continuous Insulation with Foam Sheathing. https://www.continuousinsulation.org/content/2021-ibc-irc-adopt-improved-vapor-retarder-requirements

Davidson, J. (2020, October 16). *How To Choose The Best Tiny House Insulation [Must Read]*. Tiny Living Life. https://tinylivinglife.com/2020/04/choosing-the-best-tiny-house-insulation/

Delsota, J. (2019, June 25). *Tiny House Heating And Cooling (A Complete Guide)*. Tiny House Life. https://tinyhouselife.org/tiny-house-heating-and-cooling-a-complete-guide/

Fredgaard, M. (2019, April 3). *Tiny House Humidity & Ventilation: 18 Helpful Tips (For Beginners)*. Go Downsize. https://www.godownsize.com/humidity-ventilation-tiny-houses/

Handeeman. (2016, November 25). *A/C Mini Split Installation - DIY How To Tiny House* [Video]. YouTube.

https://www.youtube.com/watch?v=AvVsbkAmuxg&feature=youtu.be

Juras, M. (2020, November 9). *The Most Popular Tiny House Air Conditioning Systems.* Tiny House Bloom. https://tinyhousebloom.com/air-conditioning-systems/

Lstiburek, J. (2015, April 15). *BSD-106: Understanding Vapor Barriers.* Building Science Corporation. https://www.buildingscience.com/documents/digests/bsd-106-understanding-vapor-barriers

Mitchell, R. (2021, February 3). *Tiny House Insulation: What I Wish I Knew When I Built My Tiny Home.* The Tiny Life. https://thetinylife.com/tiny-house-insulation/

Moore, C. (n.d.). *Which Side of the Insulation Does the Vapor Barrier Go?* Hunker. Retrieved September 9, 2021, from https://www.hunker.com/13419005/which-side-of-the-insulation-does-the-vapor-barrier-go

National Association of Home Builders, International Code Council, & Innovation Research Labs. (2015, December). *Vapor Retarders: Reducing Moisture Risk in Frame Walls.* Home Innovation Research Labs.

Ophoff, K. (2021, May 8). *Properly Venting a Tiny House.* Tiny Life Consulting. https://tinylifeconsulting.com/properly-venting-a-tiny-house/

Pollock, E. (2020, November 16). *Heating a Tiny House: 5 Tiny House Heating Options.* Powerblanket. https://www.powerblanket.com/blog/heating-a-tiny-house/

Tiny House Roof Ventilation: How To Improve Air Circulation. (2021, July 12). Super Tiny Homes. https://www.supertinyhomes.com/tiny-house-roof-ventilation-how-to-improve-air-circulation/

Tiny Nest. (2016, January 31). *Insulating a Tiny House (Ep.52)* [Video]. YouTube. https://www.youtube.com/watch?v=cJYelF7UFz4

Tumbleweed. (2020, December 5). *Insulation: A Hot and Cold Topic.* Tumbleweed Houses. https://www.tumbleweedhouses.com/insulation-a-hot-and-cold-topic/#:%7E:text=Fiberglass%3A,sufficient%20thickness%2C%20provide%20excellent%20insulation

CHAPTER 7

Bilodeau, M. (2020, March 14). *Finishing (most of) the Interior Walls and Ceiling.* TinyHome.Io. https://www.tinyhome.io/interior-walls/

Dashner Design & Restoration. (2019, February 5). *Staining Birch Plywood | *Quick Tip** [Video]. YouTube. https://www.youtube.com/watch?v=XL_58_22SEA

Davidson, J. (2020, October 16). *The No-Nonsense Guide To Tiny House Flooring Options [Complete Guide]*. Tiny Living Life. https://tinylivinglife.com/2020/04/the-best-tiny-house-flooring/

Extra Space Storage. (2021, August 24). *16 Tiny House Organization & Storage Ideas*. https://www.extraspace.com/blog/home-organization/tiny-house-organization-storage-ideas/

Hammon, D. (2019, July 8). *7 tips for decorating a tiny home*. Inhabitat - Green Design, Innovation, Architecture, Green Building. https://inhabitat.com/7-tips-for-decorating-a-tiny-home/

How to Choose Paint for your Tiny House Interior. (2020, June 2). Tiny House Giant Journey. https://tinyhousegiantjourney.com/2015/05/07/how-to-choose-paint/

Itiny. (2020, August 9). *40 Tiny House Storage and Organizing Ideas for the Entire Home*. Tiny Houses. https://www.itinyhouses.com/tiny-living/40-tiny-house-storage-organizing-ideas-entire-home/

Juras, M. (2020a, February 18). *Innovative and Clever Tiny Home Bed Solutions.* Tiny House Bloom. https://tinyhousebloom.com/tiny-home-bed-solutions/

Juras, M. (2020b, October 21). *What is the Ideal Height for a Tiny House Loft?* Tiny House Bloom. https://tinyhousebloom.com/loft-height-ideal/#:%7E:text=To%20answer%20the%20question%2C%20there,tall%20as%203'6%E2%80%9D

Langlois, S. (2018, December 24). *Here's all the space we waste in our big American homes, in one chart.* MarketWatch. https://www.marketwatch.com/story/why-the-american-dream-of-owning-a-big-home-is-way-overrated-in-one-chart-2018-05-21

Mitchell, R. (2020, August 27). *Tiny House Stairs: How To Build Them And Clever Design Ideas With Photos.* The Tiny Life. https://thetinylife.com/tiny-house-stairs/

Mulvey, K. (2018, December 20). *6 Major Dos and Don'ts of Decorating a Tiny House.* Apartment Therapy. https://www.apartmenttherapy.com/tiny-house-decorating-tips-265544

White, A. [Ana White]. (2016a, April 8). *Interior Wall and Ceiling Finish: Ana White Tiny House Build [Episode 10]* [Video]. YouTube. https://www.youtube.com/watch?v=KDwxxor7i3s

White, A. [Ana White]. (2016b, April 29). *DIY Stained Plywood Flooring: Ana White Tiny House Build [Episode 13]* [Video]. YouTube. https://www.youtube.com/watch?v=vClCx08V7ps

CHAPTER 8

Marie, M. (2018, July 31). *How to Choose the Right Tiny House Appliances.* Tiny House Society. https://www.tinysociety.co/articles/how-to-choose-tiny-house-appliances/

Plant Based Dads. (2020, March 2). *DIY IKEA TIME-LAPSE KITCHEN BUILD 2020 | COMPLETE BEFORE AND AFTER KITCHEN REMODEL in 4K* [Video]. YouTube. https://www.youtube.com/watch?v=OZD8KrqURTY

Storgaard, M. (2018, September 25). *Tiny House Furniture: 23 Brilliant Ideas You Can Steal!* Go Downsize. https://www.godownsize.com/tiny-house-furniture-small-space/